TALK LIKE AN EGYPTIAN

Key Idiomatic Expressions for Sounding Natural in Egyptian Arabic

Alaa Abou El-Nour
and
Matthew Aldrich

© 2021 by Matthew Aldrich

The author's moral rights have been asserted. All rights reserved. No part of this document may be reproduced or transmitted in any form or by any means, electronic, mechanical, photocopying, recording, or otherwise, without prior written permission of the publisher.

ISBN: 978-1-949650-49-5

Written by Alaa Abou El-Nour and Matthew Aldrich

Cover art by Duc-Minh Vu

Audio by Mohamed Shehata and Alaa Abou El-Nour

website: www.lingualism.com

email: contact@lingualism.com

Table of Contents

	page ii	**Introduction**
	page iii	**How to Use This Book**
	page iv	**Reading the Arabic Script**
Section 1	page 1	**Key Expressions**
Section 2	page 57	**Being Negative**
Section 3	page 90	**Addressing People**
Section 4	page 122	**Numbers in Idioms**
Section 5	page 151	**'God'**
Section 6	page 183	**'Hand'**

The book is divided into six sections, the first being miscellaneous items. The other sections feature themes. On the pages listed in the table above, you will find detailed tables with the segments in each section, their page numbers, and corresponding audio track numbers.

Introduction

If you're old enough, you'll remember learning to "walk like an Egyptian" back in the 1980s.* Little did you know back then that you'd be learning to talk like an Egyptian decades later!

But that's easier said than done. One of the greatest challenges in learning any language is mastering idiomatic expressions so you can sound more natural and better understand native speakers. Most learning materials–dictionaries and even course books–may present idiomatic expressions and adverbs but usually with a simple translation and little guidance on when and how to use them.

And that's why **Talk Like an Egyptian** is a unique and powerful language learning tool for **intermediate learners**. We go into depth with each word or phrase, providing detailed explanations, both literal and figurative translations, and dialogues that show you just how native speakers use it in context. We were careful to include only natural, high-frequency expressions in current use so that you can be confident in using them to sound more fluent and impress your Egyptian friends. يَلّا بينا! Let's go!

Visit the **Talk Like an Egyptian** hub at **www.lingualism.com/tle**, where you can find **free accompanying audio** to download or stream (at variable playback rates) and other resources.

---

* The American band 'The Bangles' had a number-one hit single called 'Walk Like an Egyptian' that popularized a dance with movements mimicking human poses depicted in Ancient Egyptian art.

How to Use This Book

There's really no wrong way to use this book. You can study the segments in any order or work through the book systematically. You can use the tables of contents to find a topic, or you can randomly flip to any page and learn something new.

At the beginning of each segment, you can find an icon can in the top-right corner with the corresponding audio track number on which the dialogue(s) can be found.

The segment's key word or expression appears as the title, followed by a title in English, which may be a translation that shows one meaning, or it may be a literal translation or other title to pique your interest and encourage you to read more.

Next, we give you explanations, translations, tips on usage, background information, and cultural notes to help you really understand the word or expression and how it is used in natural language.

Short dialogues show you the word or expression in context.

Extra information and useful footnotes are given in gray boxes after many dialogues.

Although the book features over 100 key words and expressions, there are hundreds more throughout the dialogues–and this is where the real value and fun comes in. By being observant and comparing the Arabic to the translations, you can learn many, many more useful idiomatic expressions, structures, interjections, adverbs, and other vocabulary.

We hope you enjoy the book and learning to TALK LIKE AN EGYPTIAN!

Reading the Arabic Script

The Arabic script is written with tashkeel (diacritics) so that you always know how to pronounce what you are reading.

At first glance, it may seem that many letters are missing diacritics, but this is by design. A final consonant is assumed to take sukuun, as Egyptian Arabic does not have case endings as Modern Standard Arabic does. We write كتاب book (and not كِتابْ). Non-final consonants without diacritics are understood to take the short vowel fatha (َ): شمس (and not شَمْسْ). This was done to keep the texts from being cluttered with redundancies and streamline fluent reading.

You can find a detailed online guide with printable PDFs on Egyptian Arabic pronunciation and Lingualism's system of orthography in the Resources section of this book's product page: www.lingualism.com/tle.

Section 1
Key Expressions

In section 1, we'll learn a variety of common everyday expressions, adverbs, and structures that will help you talk like an Egyptian. Ready?

track 001	page 2	like this	كِده
track 002	page 9	to be interested in	لُه في
track 003	page 13	'thing'	بِتاع
track 004	page 20	to "die"	مات
track 005	page 24	Believe it or not!	قال أيه
track 006	page 25	to be welcome	نوّر
track 007	page 27	Very much!	أوي أوي
track 008	page 29	Go ahead!	اِتْفضّل
track 009	page 37	outside	برّه
track 010	page 40	already	خلاص
track 011	page 46	Heavenly!	نعيماً
track 012	page 48	reasonable	معْقول
track 013	page 51	hope and faith	عشم

كِده

like this

كِده is likely the most quintessentially Egyptian word there is. Not only is it very high frequency in everyday speech, but it is unique to the Egyptian dialect. كِده is related to the Modern Standard Arabic word هكذا **like this** but takes on a range of idiomatic meanings on its own and in phrases.

Many learners make the mistake of translating **like this** literally, as زيّ ده, but this only works if you mean **such as this/him**. **If you mean to say** this way **or** in that manner, **you should use** كِده.

أ: أطلّع القميص برّه وَلّا أخلّيه زيّ ما هُوَّ جُوَّه البنْطلوْن؟

ب: لا سيبُه جُوَّه البنْطلوْن. كِده شكلُه أحْلى.

A: Should I untuck the shirt or leave it tucked into the pants?
B: No, leave it [tucked] inside. It looks better this way.

أ: هِيَّ الشّجرة بِتترسِم كِده؟
ب: أيّوَه يا حبيبي، كِده مظْبوط.

A: Is a tree drawn like this?
B: Yes, dear. That's correct.

مِش كِده functions as a question tag at the end of a sentence: '... right?', '... isn't that so?'

أ: أنا بقول نعدّي على مْحمّد بِاللّيْل بعْد الغدا أحْسن، مِش كِده؟
ب: آه يِكون أحْسن برْضُه.

A: I assume it would be better if we go by Mohamed's in the evening after lunch, wouldn't it?
B: Yes, that'd be better.

Sometimes, كِده doesn't really translate but serves to soften the sentence as a kind of filler.

أ: ها هننْزِل ولّا أيْه؟
ب: خلّينا نِستنّى كِده شْوَيّة و بعْدين نِنْزِل.

A: So, are we going out or what?
B: Let's just wait a bit, then go out.

أ: على فِكْرة، دي آخِر مرّة هشْتِـري مِنْكُم!
ب: ليْه بسّ كِده يا مدام؟

A: By the way, this is the last time I'll ever buy anything from you.
B: But why, ma'am?

كِده can refer back to something just mentioned: so, thus

أ: لازِم حدّ يِنْصح مَحْمود إنُّه يِرْجع الشُّغْل تاني.
ب: حِسيْن قالُه كِده، بسّ المُشْكِلة إنُّه مْسافِر كمان أُسْبوع.

A: Someone has to advise Mahmoud to go back to work again.
B: Hussein did [told him so]... but the problem is that he's going away in a week.

أ: أنا مِش قُلْتِلك لازِمِ تْروح لِدُكْتور قلْب؟
ب: ما أنا عمِلْت كِده فِعْلاً!

A: Didn't I tell you that you should go see a cardiologist?
B: I did [so already]!

An enthusiastic كِده!, often accompanied by a thumbs-up, describes someone or something as great, super, perfect.

أ: و البوفيْه إمْبارِح كان عامِل إزّاي في الفرح؟
ب: لأ مقولّكْش... كان كِده!

A: And how was the buffet at the wedding yesterday?
B: Just wow! It was awesome!

مقولّكْش [lit. *I won't tell you!*]

أ: الميكانيكي اللي قُلْتِلك عليه عِرِف يِصلّح عربيتِك؟
ب: مِش عايْزة أقولّك! ده طِلِع ميكانيكي أيْه! كِده!

A: Did the mechanic I told you about manage to fix the car for you?
B: You won't believe it! What a mechanic he turned out to be! Perfect!

كِده كِده **means** anyway, in any case.

أ: تِحِبّ تِفْطر دلْوَقْتي وَلّا لمّا كُلُّه يِصْحى؟
ب: لا متعْمِلوش حِسابي. أنا كِده كِده صايِم.

A: Would you like to have your breakfast now or when everyone is up?
B: No, don't count me in. I'm fasting anyway.

أ: تِحِبّي أعدّي عليْكي آخْدِك بعْد ما تْخلّصي؟
ب: لا كِده كِده مرْوَة راجْعة معايا، هتْوَصّلْني.

A: Would you like me to pick you up after you're done?
B: No, Marwa is coming back with me in any case, so she'll drive me.

The expression كِده و كِده **is used as an adverb to show that something is done as a ruse (pretending, deceiving).**

أ: أنا لَوْ ردّيْت عليْه حَيُقْعُد يِرْغي ساعْتين. أعْمِل أيْه دلْوَقْتي؟
ب: رُدّ عليْه و شوف لَوْ عايِز حاجة مُهِمّة. و لَوْ حبّيْت تِقفِّل شاوِرْلي، أرِنّ جرس الباب كِده و كِده.

A: If I pick up [answer his call], he'll talk for two hours. What should I do now?
B: Pick up and see if he needs something important. If you want to end the call, just give me a signal, and I can pretend the doorbell is ringing.

In a question, كِده وَلّا كِده **means** 'this way or that way?', 'like this or like that?'

أ: ألِفّ الطّرْحة كِده وَلّا كِده؟

ب: لا كِده أحْلى.

A: Should I wrap the headscarf like this or like this?
B: This way is better.

But in a statement, كِده وَلّا كِده **means** either way (is fine; it doesn't make a difference).

أ: تِفْتِكِري أعزّي سِليمان بِمُكالْمة وَلّا زِيارة أحْسن؟

ب: كِده وَلّا كِده، مِلْهاش لازْمة. الوَفاة عدّى عليْها كِتير، بَلاش تِقلِّب عليْه المَواجِع.

A: Do you think I can express my condolences to Soliman over the phone, or is it better if I pay him a visit?
B: Either way. There's no need to. It's been a while since the death, so don't awaken his mourning.

على كِده **means** in that case, if so.

أ: الخميس الجايّ ٦ أُكْتوبر.

ب: بِجدّ؟ على كِده مُمْكِن نِطْلع يومينْ نِغيّر جوّ في أيّ حِتّة.

A: Next Thursday is the 6th of October [an official holiday].
B: Really? In that case, we can go away somewhere [over the long weekend] for a couple of days for a change of pace.

The exclamations هِيَّ بقِت كِده؟ **and** بقى كِده؟ **mean** 'Oh, is that the way it is?'

أ: بقولّك أيْه، إنْتَ خلاص، مبقاش ليك لازْمة. أنا هخْرُج أنا و سامِح بسّ و نْسيبك بقى لْوَحْدك.

ب: بقى كِده! ماشي، بُكْرة تنْدم يا جميل!

A: You know what? You're a lost cause. I'll go hang out just with Sameh and leave you to yourself.
B: Hmm, so that's the way it is? Fine… 'Tomorrow you shall regret it, darling!'

بُكْرة تِنْدم يا جميل is a famous line from an old movie often said to make someone feel that they're going to regret it later.

When كِده **follows a number (or two consecutive numbers), it gives the meaning of approximation.**

أ: كام واحِد مِن صُحابك هَيْسافْروا معاك؟
ب: أرْبعة خمْسة كِده. لِسَّه مأكِّدْناش.

A: How many of your friends are traveling with you?
B: Around four or five. We haven't confirmed yet.

أ: كام واحِد هَييجي الحفْلة؟
ب: ييجي تلات أرْبع بنات و ولديْن تلاتة كِده.

A: How many [people] are coming to the party?
B: Around three or four girls and about two or three boys.

يِجي also shows approximation and is interchangeable with بِتاع and حَوالي here.

أ: نِتْقابِل بُكْره كام؟

ب: (على) سبْعة كِده.

A: When shall we meet tomorrow?
B: Around seven o'clock.

على, before hours, also shows approximation.

لُه في

to be interested in

أنا	لِيّا	مليش
إحْنا	لينا	ملْناش
إنْتَ	ليك	ملْكش
إنْتي	ليكي	ملْكيش
إنْتو	ليكو	ملْكوش
هُوَّ	لُه/ليه	ملوش
هِيَّ	ليها	ملْهاش
هُمّا	ليهُم	ملْهُمْش

The prepositional construction ليه [lit. to/for one] is used as a pseudo-verb meaning have as in أبويا ليه تلات إخْوات بنات. My father has three sisters. But it is also used in some common idiomatic constructions:

ليه عنْدُه [lit. to one at one] means to owe to. عنْدُه expresses the person who owes something, while ليه is the person to whom it is owed, and the construction is followed (or preceded) by what is owed.

ليْلى ليها عنْدي ١٠٠ جِنيْه.

I owe Layla 100 pounds.

أنا لِيّا ١٠٠ جِنيْه عِنْد ليْلى.

Layla owes me 100 pounds.

أ: ما تِدْفع يابني الإيجار لعمّ مُحمّد؟
ب: ما أنا لِيّا عنْدُه أصْلاً فلوس التّشْطيب.

A: Why don't you pay the rent to Uncle Mohamed?
B: Because he already owes me money for the decorations.

أ: أنا لِيّا عنْدك خُروجة بدل اللي فاتِت، خُد بالك!
ب: حاضِر والله، أوّل ما أرْجع القاهِرة هنِتْفسّح.

A: You owe me an outing to make up for last time; don't forget.
B: Absolutely! As soon as I get back to Cairo, we can go hang out.

ليه مزاج [lit. to have mood] **means** to be in the mood, feel like, crave. **It can be followed by a bare imperfect verb or ل with a noun.**

أ: عايِز حاجة و أنا جايّ مِن برّه؟
ب: آه يا ريْت! لِيّا مزاج آكُل آيْس كْريم أوي. هاتْلي و إنْتَ راجِع.

A: Do you want anything while I'm on my way back home?
B: Yes, please! I really feel like eating ice cream. Bring me some on your way back.

أ: ما تيجي نِطْلع يوْميْن السّاحِل.
ب: لا مليش مزاج خالِص لِبحْر اليوْميْن دوْل.

A: Why don't we go to the coast for a couple of days?
B: No, I'm not at all in the mood for the sea these days.

The construction ليه في means to be interested in or to be into (something).

أ: ليك في أفْلام الأكْشِن؟

ب: آه لِيّا. لِيْه؟

أ: ما تيجي نِدْخُل سينِما! فيه فيلْم حِلْو أوي لِسّه نازِل.

A: Are you into action movies?
B: Yeah, I am. Why?
A: Let's go to the movies then! A really cool movie has just come out.

أ: تِحِبّي لِبّ أبْيَض وَلّا أسْمَر؟

ب: لا أنا مليش في اللِّبّ خالِص.

A: Would you like white or yellow [snacking] seeds?
B: No thanks, I don't care for seeds at all.

Depending on the context, the same construction can also mean to be one's business/concern.

أ: أنا مِش فاهِم هُمّا مِش مُوافْقين ليْه على عريس زيْنب.

ب: و إنْتَ ليك أيْه في المَوْضوع ده عشان تِقول رأيُك فيه.

A: I don't get why they don't accept Zeinab's groom's proposal.
B: And what business is it of yours to give an opinion on it?

أ: بقولّك أيْه، ما تْحاوِل تِقْنع بابا بِـمَوْضوع سفري في الصّيْف.

ب: مليش فيه يا حبيبي. المَوْضوع ده بِتاعك.

A: Hey! Why don't you try to convince dad of me going traveling in the summer?

B: It's none of my concern, bro... This issue is yours.

بِتاع

'thing'

بِتاع is technically a noun but has adapted an idiomatic usage that makes it harder to classify. It has three forms—masculine, feminine, and plural—which agree with the noun it refers to. We can divide its usage into two main groups: 1) a connecting word for possession or association; and 2) a placeholder name.

m.	بِتاع
f.	بِتاعة
pl.	بِتوع

بِتاع expresses 'belonging,' whether that is literal possession (ownership) or association in the speaker's mind. It can best be thought of as meaning of.

العربية بِتاعةِ الرّاجِل جِديدة.

The man's car is new.
[lit. The car <u>of</u> the man – new]

Notice that the word for 'car' is feminine in Egyptian Arabic, so the feminine form بِتاعة is required. And because it is technically the first part of a construct phrase (idaafa) with the following noun, the ending is pronounced ةِ -it.

بِتاع can also be followed by a pronoun suffix. In this case, it is more or less interchangeable with a noun taking a pronoun suffix directly: الكِتاب بِتاعي = كِتابي my book. But because the phrase with بِتاع is a longer construction, possession is somewhat emphasized.

مكْتبي آخِر الطُّرْقة على الشِّمال.

<u>My office</u> is at the end of the corridor on the left.

المكْتب بِتاعي آخِر الطُّرْقة على الشِّمال.

<u>My (own) office</u> is at the end of the corridor on the left.

In Egyptian Arabic, relatively recently borrowed or phonetically strange (non-Arabic-sounding) foreign loan words cannot take possessive pronoun suffixes, in which case the only option is a construction with بِتاع. Which foreign words are acceptable to use with possessive pronoun suffixes may seem arbitrary, so it's best to listen to how Egyptians use them. For example, the word لابْتوب is still seen to be an English word being used in everyday speech among Egyptians, so it sounds odd to the Egyptian ear to add a possessive pronoun suffix directly to it.

أ: فيْن اللّابْتوْب بِتاعك؟
ب: جُوّه على السِّرير.

A: Where's <u>your laptop</u>?
B: Inside, on the bed.

لاِبْتاوبك is little used and would sound odd to most Egyptians.

However, موبايْل [lit. mobile] cell phone has been normalized in Egyptian Arabic; that is, it is now seen as an Egyptian Arabic word, so it can take a possessive pronoun suffix.

حدّ شاف الموبايل بِتاعي؟ = حدّ شاف موبايْلي؟

Has anyone seen my cell phone?

بِتاع can be used without a preceding noun when that referent is understood.

أ: هُوَّ الجَاكيت ده بِتاعك وَلاّ بِتاع أَحْمد؟
ب: لا مِش بِتاع حدّ مِنِّنا. ده بِتاع السبّاك اللي جهْ إمْبارِح.

A: Is this jacket <u>yours</u> or <u>Ahmed's</u>?
B: It's neither of ours. It belongs to the plumber who came yesterday.

أ: المسْطرة دي بِتاعْتي. أُمّال دي بِتاعِةْ مين؟
ب: بِتاعْتي، بِتاعْتي!

A: This ruler is mine. And whose is this one?
B: Mine! It's mine!

بِتاع is also used to show belonging, but not necessarily ownership.

أ: فيْن المُفْتاح بِتاع العِلْبة دي؟
ب: هتْلاقيه في الدُرْج عنْدك.

A: Where's the key for [that belongs to] this box?
B: You'll find it there in the drawer.

بِتاع is also used to clarify 'which one' is meant by associating the thing or person with a place, time, etc.

أ: بفكّر أكلِّم شيْماء أسْألْها على فُنْدُق في بورْسعيد.
ب: شيْماء مين؟
أ: شيْماء بِتاعةْ مُعسْكر السّنة اللي فاتِت.

A: I'm thinking of calling Shaimaa to ask her about a hotel in Port Said.
B: Shaimaa who?
A: Shaimaa from camp last year.

أ: عارِف قابِلْت مين النّهارْده!
ب: مين؟
أ: أحْمد شعْبان بِتاع صيْدلة.
ب: ياه بِتاع زمان!

A: Guess who I ran into today!
B: Who?
A: Ahmed Shaban from the faculty of pharmacy.
B: Woah! From way back when!

Similar to the associative usage above, بِتاع can refer to someone who performs a job when no official word exists (that you know of) for that profession. For example, a delivery guy is بِتاع الدِّليفري. It is not preceded by a noun, but the inferred noun reference would be راجِل man. For a woman, it would be بِتاعِة.

أ: إدّيْت بقْشيش لِبْتاع الدِّليفري؟
ب: آه إدّيتُهْ ٥ جِنيْهْ.

A: Did you give a tip to the delivery guy?
B: Yeah, I gave him 5 LE.

أ: عدّي و إنْتي راجْعة على بْتاع الخُضار، هاتيلي كيلو طماطِم.
ب: حاضِر.

A: On your way home, pass by the greengrocer's [the vegetable guy] and bring me a kilo of tomatoes.
B: Okay.

Here are more 'associative' unofficial job titles that mention what the person works with (makes, installs, repairs, sells, etc.). These are also used to refer to the shop where the service is provided.

بِتاع الإزاز glass installer/vendor/manufacturer

بِتاع الأسانسير elevator operator

بِتاع الألوميتال window installer

بِتاع الجِنوط car tire vendor/installer

بِتاع الخُضار vegetable vendor

بِتاع الرخام marble installer/vendor/manufacturer

بِتاع الدِّليفري delivery person

بِتاع الستاير blinds installer/vendor
بِتاع العجل bicycle vendor/repairman
بِتاع العيش bread vendor
بِتاع الفول ful (bean) vendor

The second main usage of بِتاع is as a placeholder name when you don't know, can't remember, or don't want to mention the word for something: thing, thingy, thingamajigger, whatchamacallit, doohickey, **etc. It is usually followed by a demonstrative pronoun. The feminine form is** البِتاعة دي, **which a native speaker might use when they suspect the noun in question is feminine, whether that is because the word is on the tip of their tongue, or they are making an association with another word subconsciously.**

m.	البِتاع ده
f.	البِتاعة دي
pl.	البِتوع دول

أ: أحْمد، ناوِّلْني البِتاع اللي على التّرابيْزة.
ب: خُدي!

A: Ahmed, hand me the thingy on the table.
B: Here!

أ: فيْن البِتاعة اللي كنّا رابْطين بيها الصّنْدوق؟
ب: الدُّبارة؟ رميْتها.

A: Where's the whatchamacallit we were tying the box with?
B: The string? I threw it out.

أ: عارْفة البِتاع ده اللي بِتِلْبِسيه على راسِك في الشِّتا؟

ب: تُقصُّدي الزَّعْبوط؟
أ: أَيْوَه، هاتيلي واحِد.

A: You know that thing you wear on your head in the winter?
B: You mean a 'stocking cap'?
A: Yes, bring me one of those.

أ: عايْزة أشْتِري البِتوع دوْل اللي بيتْرِكِّبوا في السَّتايِر.
ب: الحلقات؟
أ: لا، اللي بتْشِدّي السِّتارة مِنْهُم.

A: I want to buy some of those thingies that attach to curtains.
B: The rings?
A: No, the things you pull the curtains by.

أ: كُنْت ماشْيَة إمْبارِح في شارِع... اااااه... بِتاع ده...
ب: يا بِنْتي ما تُرَكِّزي!
أ: الشَّارِع اللي كُنّا فيه الشَّهْر اللي فات.

A: Yesterday, I was walking down... uh–what is it–Street... um...
B: Focus, girl!
A: That street we were just on last month.

At the end of a sentence, و بِتاع can be used to imply that related items or actions are included: and so on / et cetera / and whatnot.

أ: عملْت أيْه إمْبارِح في الإنْترڤْيو؟
ب: رُحْت و سألوني عن السّي ڤي و قالولي هَيْكلِّموني و بِتاع.

A: What did you do at the interview yesterday?
B: I went, and they asked me about my CV, told me they'd call me, and so on.

مات

to "die"

Of course, the verb مات literally means to die. But just like its English translation, it is used metaphorically in a number of idioms.

In a construction with مات plus و plus a bare imperfect verb, it means to be dying to (do), as in really want to (do).

أ: الواحِد تِعِب مِن كُتر الزِّيارات العائِلية.
ب: يا راجِل! ده إنْتَ كُنْت هتْموت و تِرْجع مصْر علشان عيلْتك.

A: I'm really tired of all the family gatherings.
B: Come on! You were dying to get back to Egypt for your family.

When the complement of the verb is a noun, it is governed by the preposition في. مات في: to die for, be crazy about.

أ: هتِعْمليلْنا أيْه ع َالغدا؟
ب: فتّة. أحْمد بيْموت فيها.

A: What are you going to make us for lunch?
B: Fatteh. Ahmed is crazy about it.

أ: بِتحِبّي تِسْمعي مين؟
ب: بموت في كايْروكي.

A: Who do you listen to?
B: I adore [the rock band] Cairokee.

But when the governed noun is جِلْدُه one's skin, another meaning is understood. مات في جِلْدُه [lit. to die in one's skin] means to be scared to death.

أ: شُفْت الحرامي اللي مِسْكوه؟
ب: آه، أمّا شاف البوليس مات في جِلْدُه. شكْلُه أوِّل مرّة يِسْرق.

A: Did you see the thief they caught?
B: Yes, when he saw the police, he was scared to death. It seems like it's his first time stealing.

مات مِن to die from **can be either metaphorical hyperbole or literal, depending on the context.**

أ: أنا هموت من التَّعب خلاص. مِش مُمْكِن الضَّغْط ده كُلُّه!
ب: معلِشّ، هانِت. الامْتِحانات قرَّبِت تِخْلَص.

A: I'm going to die from exhaustion. All of this stress is unbelievable!
B: Don't worry. We're almost there. The exams are almost over.

أ: لَوْ عِرفْت اللي حصلّي إمْبارِح هتْموت مِن الضَّحْك.
ب: ليْه؟ أيْه اللي حصل؟

A: If you knew what happened to me yesterday, you'd die laughing.
B: Why? What happened?

مات مِن الجوع [lit. to die of hunger] **and** كان ميِّت مِن الجوع [lit. to be dead from hunger] **mean** to starve to death, to be starving. **Of course, it's usually hyperbole, meaning** to be extremely hungry. مِن الجوع **can be omitted when the meaning remains clear from the context.**

أ: إنْتَ جايّ إمْتى يا عمرو؟
ب: خمس دقايِق. جهِّزيلي بسّ الأكْل علشان ميِّت (مِ الجوع)!

A: When will you arrive, Amr?
B: In five minutes. Prepare some food for me. I'm starving!

In the dialogue above, ميِّت can be replaced by مُتّ *I died* or هموت *I will die*.

مِن الـ = مِ الـ

أ: يا نْهار أبْيَض! أُسْتاذ سعيد كمان اِتْوَفّى؟
ب: آه شُفْت؟ الرّاجِل مات مِن القهْرة بعْد مِراتُه على طول.

A: Oh my God! Mr. Said passed away, too?
B: Yeah, can you believe it? The man died from grief right after his wife [died].

مات على القرْش [lit. to die over a penny] **means** to be very stingy (with money).

أ: اِسْتِلْفي مِن خالتِك.
ب: مين؟! دي بِتْموت عَ القرْش.

A: Borrow [money] from your aunt.
B: Who?! She's so stingy!

The noun موْت death **as an adverb of intensity is synonymous with** جِدًّا **and** أوي **very.**

أ: ألْبِس الأحْمر ولّا الإسْوِد؟
ب: الإسْوِد... شيك موْت!

A: Shall I wear the red one or the black one?
B: The black one is extremely elegant!

وَحشْتيني موْت!

I missed you so badly!

قال أيْه

Believe it or not!

Believe it or not, قال أيْه [lit. said what] **is used to show amazement, bewilderment, or disbelief.**

أ: هُوَّ صحيح دُكْتور محمّد اِسْتقال؟
ب: آه، مِن غيرِ أيّ مُقدِّمات... قال أيْه، جاله عرْض أفْضل في مكان تاني.

A: Is it true that Dr. Mohamed resigned?
B: Yes, and without any warning. Believe it or not, he's been granted a better offer somewhere else.

أ: هِيَّ طنْط سُعاد مجتْش الفرح ليْه؟
ب: قال أيْه، كانِت ناسْيَة المعاد... بسّ حِجج فارْغة طبْعاً.

A: Why didn't auntie Soaad attend the wedding?
B: She claims she forgot the date... but that's nonsense [lit. empty excuses], of course.

نَوَّر

to be welcome

نَوَّر, which literally means to illuminate, light up, is used for welcoming guests. That is, you can welcome guests by letting them know that they have "illuminated" your home.

The host tells the arriving guest(s) you have illuminated me نـي or us نـا نوّرْت(ي/وا). The guest then replies with a set response, implying that the home is, in fact, illuminated by the host.

أ: أَهْلاً أَهْلاً يا حبيبْتي نوَّرْتونا!
ب: مِنوَّر بيكو يا حبيبي!

A: Welcome, dear! You've illuminated us [our home].
B: [The house] is illuminated by you, dear!

مِنوَّر is invariable (always masculine singular) because it refers to the home (not the addressee). It is followed by بيك or by بِنورك by your light (which can also be feminine or plural, depending on the addressee). You can also omit مِنوَّر and just ay بِنورك.

You can have the same exchange at the end of a visit.

(The host politely indicates that it's time for the guest to go.)

أ: أنا مِش هَمْسِك فيكي عشان الوَقْت اِتْأَخّر... بسّ وَاللهِ نَوّرْتِيني يا نادْيَة.

ب: (مِنوّر) بِنورِك يا حبيبْتي.

A: I won't hold you up, as it's getting late... but you really illuminated me [my home], Nadya.
B: (It's illuminated) with your light, dear.

It might also be said jokingly to a friend who is visiting if the electricity goes out. (In this case, it does refer to the addressee and so is variable for gender and number.)

أ: أيْه اللي حصل؟

ب: النّور قطع... مِنوّر يا حبيبي!

أ: يا عمّ اُسْكُت بقى... هنْذاكِر إزّاي دِلْوَقْتي؟!

A: What happened?
B: The power went out... You're illuminating, buddy!
A: Shut up, man... How are we going to study now?!

In the bare imperfect tense (rather than the perfect tense), the verb تِنوّر (or its feminine or plural form) can be used to extend an invitation or let someone know they are welcome to visit.

أ: إزّيِّك يا طنْط، ماما كانِت باعْتالِك حاجة معايا. ينْفع أعدّيها عليْكي بُكْره؟

ب: طبْعاً يا حبيبي! تِنوّر في أيّ وَقْت.

A: Hi, auntie! Mom gave me something to give to you. Can I bring it by tomorrow?
B: Of course, honey. You are more than welcome anytime!

أوي أوي

Very much!

أوي is an adverb that follows an adjective in Egyptian Arabic to mean very: كِبير أوي very big. It can also follow a verb to mean very much, really.

أ: أنا بحِبّ المانْجة.

ب: و أنا برْضُه. بحِبّها أوي!

A: I like mangoes.
B: Me, too! I really like them!

But to show even more emphasis in a playful, somewhat exaggerated style, you can simply double it up: أوي أوي

أ: عجبِتْكو تُرْكِيا؟

ب: أوي أوي، تِجنِّن!

A: Did you guys like Turkey?
B: So much! It's amazing!

أوي أوي can also mean *of course,* in the same playful tone, to show that you are able and willing to comply with a request.

أ: ماما، مُمْكِن تِحضّريلي الشّنْطة؟

ب: أوي أوي يا حبيبي، مِن عينَيا!

A: Mom, could you pack my bag?
B: Of course, dear! With pleasure!

In the dialogue above, the mother could also respond with آه طِبْعاً، أوي أوي! Yes, of course!

اِتْفَضَّل

Go ahead!

This common expression is used in many situations, as seen in the dialogues below. It basically gives someone the go-ahead to do something. As it is an imperative verb–literally meaning be so kind (as to...)–it has three forms, depending on the person being spoken to. To one man, you say اِتْفَضَّل; to a woman, اِتْفَضَّلي, and to more than one person, اِتْفَضَّلوا.

m.	اِتْفَضَّل
f.	اِتْفَضَّلي
pl.	اِتْفَضَّلوا

اِتْفَضَّل is said when handing someone something or giving them permission to take it: Go ahead. / Help yourself. / Here you are.

أ: مُمْكِن واحْدة؟
ب: اِتْفَضَّل!

A: May I have one?
B: Go ahead!

أ: معاك بقية خمْسين؟
ب: آه معايا فكّة. اتْفضّلي.

A: Do you have change for a fifty [-pound bill]?
B: Yes, I have change. Here you are.

أ: يا صباح الخيرْ... اتْفضّلوا!
ب: أيْه ده؟ دي بِـمُناسْبةْ أيْه الشّوكولاتة دي؟
أ: بِـمُناسْبةْ التّرْقية.
ب: ألْف مبْروك و بِالتّوْفيق إن شاء الله!

A: Good morning, (folks!) Here you are!
B: What's this? What occasion are the chocolates for?
A: For [on the occasion of] my promotion.
B: Congratulations! And wishing you success, God willing!

اتْفضّل is used in giving someone permission to enter, exit, pass by, or take a seat.

أ: سلام عليْكم يا دكْتور. إزّي حضْرتك؟
ب: و عليْكُم السّلام و رحْمةْ اللّه... اتْفضّلي!

A: Hello, doctor. How are you doing?
B: Hello! Please come in.

أ: مِن فضْلك، مُمْكِن أعدّي؟
ب: آه طبْعاً اتْفضّلي! معلِشّ مخدْتِش بالي.

A: Excuse me, can I get by?
B: Oh, of course. There you go! Sorry, I didn't notice.

(a passenger in a taxi or on a microbus)

أ: على إيدك هِنا ياسْطى اللّه يِبارِكْلك!

ب: اِتْفضّل يا باشا.

A: [Stop] anywhere here please, driver! Thank you!
B: Here you are, sir!

(a host welcoming guests into her home)

أ: أهْلاً و سهْلاً نوّرْتونا.

ب: مِنوّر بِصْحابُه حبيبْتي.

أ: اِتْفضّلوا عَ السُّفْرة على طول بقى، الأكْل خلاص جاهِز.

A: Welcome! You brought us light [to our home].
B: It's already illuminated by its owners.
A: Come in! Straight to the dining table. The food is ready.

اِتْفضّل can give someone permission to proceed to do something or to carry on with what they were doing: Go ahead!; You first!

أ: على فِكْرة، أنا مُمْكِن أخلّص الشُّغْلانة دي في خمس دقايِق.

ب: والله؟ طبّ اِتْفضّل، وَرّينا شطارْتك!

A: By the way, I can fix this in five minutes.
B: Really? Okay, go ahead and show us your skills.

In the dialogue above, the second speaker is skeptical, so he invites (almost dares) the other person to demonstrate his skills.

أ: هِيَّ المكنة شغّالة؟
ب: آه ثَواني بسّ، بخلّص آخِر حاجة.
أ: اِتْفضّل، خُد وَقْتك.
ب: شُكْراً لِذوْقك... اِتْفضّل حضْرِتك، أنا خلّصْت خلاص.

A: Is the [ATM] machine working?
B: Yes, just a moment, and I'll be finished.
A: Okay, go ahead and take your time.
B: Thanks for your courtesy... Go ahead, sir. I'm done.

In the dialogue above, اِتْفضّل is used as a courtesy to let the other person go first. Sometimes people say this back and forth to each other, insisting the other go first.

أ: بسّ فيه حاجة مُهِـ...
ب: المُشْكِلة إنّ المشْروع كِده مُمْكِن... كُنْت عايِز تِقول حاجة؟
أ: لأ لأ اِتْفضّل حضْرِتك.
ب: لأ قول إنْتَ فِكْرِتك و أنا هكمِّل بعْدك... اِتْفضّل.

A: But there's an important thi...
B: The problem is the project might... you wanted to say something?
A: No, no. It's okay. You go ahead.
B: No, you tell your thoughts, and I'll continue afterward... go ahead.

اِتْفضّل can be used to ask someone to leave.

أ: أيْه ده؟ إنْتَ أيْه اللي جابك هِنا؟

ب: أبْدا. أنا كُنْت عايِز أشوفك.

أ: مِش عايْزة أقابِل حدّ. اِتْفضّل مِن هِنا لوْ سمحْت.

A: What's this? What brought you here?
B: Nothing. I just wanted to see you.
A: I don't want to see anyone. Please, go away.

A blunt, aggressive expression to tell someone to leave is اِتْفضّل مِن غيْر مطْرود Leave before I kick you out! [lit. without being kicked out]

Sometimes, اِتْفضّل is used as a polite gesture, but it is not a genuine invitation and should not be taken literally. In this context, it is usually said as a greeting or response to a greeting, for example, when you meet someone you know in the street near your place, from a distance when you are driving or walking by. It literally gives the sense of 'Please, come join me, since we've met!' **but the invitation is normally declined.**

(by a shopkeeper to someone passing by on the street)

أ: سلامُ عليْكو يا حاجّ أحْمد!

ب: سلامٌ و رحْمةُ اللّه! اِتْفضّل!

A: Hello, hajj Ahmed!
B: Hello! Join me!

(by someone in front of their building whose friend has just passed by to give them something quickly but wasn't planning to stay to visit)

أ: بِجدّ مِش عارْفة أشْكُرِك إزّاي. إنْتي أنْقذْتيني بِالكِتاب دَه.

ب: لا يا بِنْتي، متْقوليش كِده. إنْتي على طريقي أصْلاً و دي نُسْخة زِيادة معايا... أنا معملتْش حاجة.

أ: تِسْلمي بِجدّ! طب اِتْفضّلي طيّب مِش هنفْضل واقْفين في الشّارِع كِده.

ب: لأ والله يادوْب ألْحق أرْكب و أروّح.

A: Seriously, I don't know how to thank you. You saved me with this book.
B: No, honey, don't say that. You were already on my way, and I have an extra copy. It's nothing.
A: Thanks, really! Well, come up, please. We can't keep standing like this in the street.
B: No, I have to be getting home.

(by someone driving who sees an acquaintance walking down the street)

أ: دُكْتور مُجيب! إزّي حضْرِتك؟

ب: هُوَّ إنْتَ اللي عمّال تِضْرب كلاكْس!

أ: اِتْفضّل طيّب أوَصّل حضْرِتك.

ب: تِسْلم يا حبيبي، أنا رايِح لِمكان آخِر الشّارِع ده.

A: Dr. Mogeeb! How are you doing?
B: Ah, that's you who's honking!
A: Get in, please. I'll give you a lift.
B: Bless you! [No need...] I'm just heading somewhere at the end of this street.

اِتْفَضّل, used with a pronoun suffix, is a common response to compliments about possessions, especially clothing and accessories. It literally means 'here, take it!' but should not be taken literally, of course!

أ: حِلْو أوي القميص ده عليْك.
ب: ربِّنا يِخلّيك يا حمادة، اِتْفَضّلهُ!

A: That shirt looks really cool on you!
B: Oh, thanks, Hamada! Here, take it!

أ: ما شاء الله حِلْوة أوي السّاعة دي حبيبْتي.
ب: اِتْفَضّليها يا طنْط.
أ: تِسْلمي يا قمر.

A: Wow! That's a really nice watch, honey.
B: Here you are, auntie!
A: Thanks, sweetie!

Sometimes اِتْفَضّل is used sarcastically when you are disappointed or surprised by something, in the sarcastic sense of 'Here we go [again]!'

أ: تخيِّلي الرّاجِل البِجِح سارِقٍ كهْربا مِن العِمارة و جايّ يِتْخانِق معايا فكرْني أنا اللي بلّغْت عنُّه.
ب: اِتْفَضّل! أهُه ده اللي ناقِص كمان... فِعْلاً اللي اخْتشوا ماتوا! ناس غريبة!

A: Can you imagine this insolent man stole electricity from the whole building and came to fight with me thinking I'm the one who reported him.

B: Here we go! This is really what was missing... Indeed 'those who were shy died!' Such weird people!

اللي اِخْتشوا ماتوا (idiom) [lit. *those who were shy died*] describes <u>brazen, shameless people</u>. The idiom can be traced back to a fire at a public bathhouse in the late 1800s in Egypt. Women who ran out of the bathhouse naked survived the fire while those too embarrassed to run out naked perished.

أ: اِتْفضَّلي ياخْتي... أهُه الطَّيَران كُلُّه وِقِف و مِش هنِعْرف نِسافِر في حِتَّة.

ب: يا دي الحظّ المِنيِّل! ده أنا ما صدَّقْت الأجازة ظبَّطْتها.

A: Here we go, sis! All flights have been suspended, and we won't be able to travel anywhere.

B: What nasty luck! I could barely arrange the vacation.

بَرَّه

outside

The basic meaning of بَرَّه **is** outside (of a room or building).

أ: عايِز ألْبِس.
ب: أطْلع بَرَّه يَعْني؟
أ: آه مِن فضْلك.

A: I want to get dressed.
B: You mean I should get out?
A: Yes, please.

أ: بُصّي أنا مِسْتنّياكي في مدْخل العمارة عشان نِطْلع سَوا. هتْلاقي العمارة في وِشّ وَرْشةْ ميكانيكا.
ب: اطْلعيلي بَرَّه طيِّب عشان أشوفك. أنا في أوِّل الشّارِع أهُه.

A: Listen, I'm waiting for you at the building entrance so that we can go up together. You'll find the building right across from the mechanic's.

B: Come outside then, so I can see you. I'm at the beginning of the street.

أ: يا جماعة، يَلّا نُخْرُج شُوَيّة.

ب: نِروح فينْ؟

أ: أيّ حِتّة برّه نِشِمّ هَوا.

A: Hey guys, let's go out
B: Where shall we go?
A: Anywhere outside so we can breathe the fresh air.

It can also mean out [and about], **as in** not at home, **but not necessarily literally outside [on the street].**

أ: إنْتي في البيْت النّهارْده؟

ب: لا أنا برّه طول النّهار.

A: Are you at home today?
B: No, I'll be out all day.

In certain contexts, برّه **(or** برّه مصر**) can mean** abroad.

أ: هتِعْمِل أيْه بعْد ما تْخلّص كلّية إن شاء اللّه؟

ب: عايِز أسافِر برّه مصْر أكمّل ماجِسْتيرْ.

A: What are you going to do after you finish college, God willing?
B: I want to go abroad to get a master's.

أ: أيْه ده؟ حِلْو أوي البرْفيوم بِتاعِك.

ب: يا بِنْتي ده الأصْلي بِتاع برّه. لازِم يِكون حِلْو، اتْفضّليه!

A: Oh! Your perfume smells great.
B: Yeah, dear. It's the original from abroad. It'd better [be great]. Take it, please!

أ: برّه الفُرص أكْتر بِكْتير و الحَياة أسْهل مِن هِنا.
ب: بِيتهيّألك! يابْني كُلّ مكان و لُه طبيعْتُه. برّه الحَياة رِتْمها أسْرع بِكْتير مِن هِنا و مُتطلّباتها أكْتر.

A: Abroad, there are so many more opportunities, and life is easier than here.
B: That's what you think. Dude, every place has its own nature. Life abroad is much faster-paced than here and is more demanding.

You may also hear the phrase بِلاد برّه abroad from working-class and rural Egyptians.

أ: متعرفْش مسْعود إبْن الحاجّ صابِر فيْن أراضيه دِلْوَقْتي؟
ب: بِيْقولوا هاجِر بِلاد برّه.

A: Do you happen to know where on earth hajj Saber's son Massoud is now?
B: They say he emigrated abroad.

The expression مِن برّه برّه means direct, straight—from one place to another without going home, etc., in between.

أ: مها إنْتي جايّة عَ الغدا؟
ب: لا يا ماما، هاروح أجيب الفُسْتان مِن برّه برّه.

A: Maha, are you coming home for lunch?
B: No, mom. I'll go straight to get the dress.

خلاص

already

خلاص is used both as an adverb and an interjection. Although it can be translated in many ways depending on the context, it basically expresses that something is already done. It shares a root with the verbs خِلِص to come to an end **and** خلّص to finish.

As an adverb, خلاص can precede or follow a verb, or it can be used in isolation in a short answer.

أ: مُمْكِن أطْلُب بيتْزا مارْجريتا عَ السّريع؟
ب: شطّبْنا خلاص، معلِشّ.

A: Can I order one Margherita pizza quickly?
B: We've wrapped up [closed] already. Sorry.

أ: أخْبار وَرق اِمْتِحانات التّاريخ أيْه؟
ب: أُسْتاذ محمّد خلاص صحّح كلّ الوَرق، متِقْلقْش.

A: What's up with the history exam papers?
B: Mr. Mohamed has already corrected all the sheets. Don't worry.

أ: خلّصْت الواجِب بِتاعك؟

ب: آه خلاص.

A: Have you finished your homework?
B: Yes, all done.

أ: أخْبار الخُطوبة أيْه؟

ب: لا خلاص... المَوْضوع ده خِلِص مِن بدْري.

A: How is the engagement going?
B: Oh, no... that ended a long time ago.

أ: قُدّامك قدّ أيْه و تْخلّص علشان نِمْشي؟

ب: خلاص باقيلي مُكالْمة واحْدة و أقْفِل النّهارْده.

A: How much more do you have left to do before we can leave?
B: It's [almost] over. I just have one phone call left to wrap up for today.

خلاص can be used to decline an offer, implying that you've had enough already.

أ: أعْمِلُّكم شاي؟

ب: لا خلاص كِده... أنا مفيش مكان في مِعْدِتي خلاص!

A: Shall I make you tea?
B: No, no need! I don't have any more room in my stomach!

خلاص can be used to tell someone to stop: Enough is enough!

(a father and his two sons)

أ: الِبْسوا يَلّا علشان نِنْزِل.

ب: بسّ حازِم ضربْني!

ج: لأ هُوَّ اللي ابْتدى!

أ: بسّ خلاص ، الِبْسوا بقولُّكو.

A: Get dressed. We're going out.
B: But Hazem hit me!
C: No, he started it!
A: Knock it off! I said, 'Get dressed!'

أ: أنا قُلْتِلك ميةْ مرّة كان لازِم تِسيب الشُّغْل ده مِن زمان.

ب: ما خلاص بقى! هتِفْضلوا تْقولولي كِده لِحدّ إمْتى؟ أهُه اللي حصل!

A: I told you a hundred times, you should have left this job a long time ago.
B: Enough already! How long will you keep telling me that? What's done is done!

خلاص can be used to calm someone down or reassure them that it's not a big deal. In this usage, it is often interchangeable with **معلِشّ** but is less empathetic–more matter of fact.

أ: شُفْتي الغبي ده خبط العربية إزّاي! والله ما هسيبُه!

ب: خلاص حصل خير. ده خدْش بسيط. و إحْنا مِش فاضْيين.

A: Did you see how this idiot bumped the car?! I swear I won't let him off!
B: It's okay, no big deal. It's just a simple scratch, and we don't have time.

أ: مالك بسّ فيه أيْه؟

ب: ما اتْقبلتِش في المِنْحة. لِسّه باعْتينْلي حالاً.

أ: خَلاص وَلا يْهمّك... خيرْها في غيرْها إن شاء الله.

A: What's wrong with you? What happened?
B: I didn't get the scholarship. They just sent me [this].
A: It's okay. Never mind. Hopefully, a better chance will come along.

أ: لَوْ تِحِبّ أخلّيه يِيجي و يِعْتِذِرْلك هِنا قُدّامْهُم كُلّهِم.

ب: لأ خَلاص المِسامِح كَريم. المَوْضوع مِش مِسْتاهِل كُلّ ده.

A: If you want, I can make him come and apologize to you in front of them.
B: No, it's okay. Better to forgive and forget. It's not worth it.

المِسامح كريم (proverb) [lit. he who forgives is generous]

لا خَلاص is a common response used in making payments. A customer can say it to mean 'Keep the change.' However, when a server or shopkeeper says it–although it means 'No need to pay.'–it should not be taken literally. This is a customary polite response. It does not mean that the meal or item is free. Ask to pay again! It can also be used to insist on paying between friends or acquaintances.

أ: فوِّلّي التّانْك مِن فضْلك بنْزين ٩٢.
ب: ٣٤٨ جِنيْهْ.
أ: ماشي اتْفضّل.
ب: ثَواني أجيبْلِك فكّة.
أ: لا خلاص تمام كِده.

A: Fill up the tank with 92[-grade] gas, please.
B: That's 348 LE.
A: Okay, here you are.
B: Just a moment. I'll bring you your change.
A: No, that's all right. [Keep it.]

أ: الحِساب كامْ؟
ب: لا خلاص خلّي يا أُسْتاذة، عيْب!

A: How much is the check?
B: No, that's okay, ma'am. Keep it, please!

خلّي is not to be taken literally. It is merely a figure of speech embedded in the language and reflects the importance of hospitality in Egyptian culture. Think of it simply as a humble thank-you. You are still expected to pay!

أ: شوف بقالْنا قدّ أيْه بِنْحاوِل نِرتِّب خُروجة!
ب: بسّ الحمْدُ لِلّه عِرِفْنا نُخْرُج في الآخِر.
أ: إنْتَ بِتِعْمِل أيْه؟

ب: لا خلاص المرّة دي عليّا يا أُسْتاذ. اِبْقى حاسِب إنْتَ الخُروجة اللي جايّة بقى.

A: We'd been trying to meet up for so long!
B: But thank God, we finally did it.
A: What are you doing?!
B: No, it's done. This time it's on me, mister! You can pay next time.

خلاص و **is used at the end of a statement to mean** and that's that, **putting an end to any potential argument:** End of discussion! / That's that!

أ: عمِلْتي أيْه في تقْديم مدْرِسةْ كريم؟
ب: المَوْضوع طِلِع مُتْعِب أوي. أنا هدخِّلُه مدْرِسةْ أخوه و خلاص.

A: What did you do about school admission for Karim?
B: It turned out to be very exhausting. I will enroll him in his brother's school, and that's that.

أ: مِش هتْفكّر في عقْد السُّعودية ده؟
ب: والله فكّرْت فيه... بسّ الدِّنْيا هتِتْلخْبط جامِد.
أ: طبّ هتِعْمِل أيْه؟
ب: هكمِّل في شُغْلي هِنا و خلاص. كلُّها مُحصَّلة بعْضها.

A: Won't you consider the Saudi contract?
B: Honestly, I did, but it'd be such an ordeal.
A: What will you do then?
B: I'll stay on with my job here, and that's that. It's all the same at the end of the day.

نَعيماً

Heavenly!

نَعيماً is a greeting to someone in two specific situations, as we will see below. It comes from the word نعيم dwelling, which is one of the names of Paradise, so it implies 'feel as if you're in heaven.' The response to this greeting is الله يِنْعِم عليْك 'May God grant you a dwelling in heaven.'

نَعيماً is said to a man who has just recently had a haircut or shave. It is what a man's barber will say after he finishes cutting his hair and what you can say to someone you notice has a fresh haircut.

أ: نعيما يا باشا!
ب: اللّه يِنْعِم عليْك يا حبيبي، حِسابْنا كام؟

A: Feel in heaven, Pasha!
B: May God give you heaven, dear. How much do I owe you?

أ: نَعيماً يا دَرْش!
ب: اللّه يِنْعِم عليْك... حِلْوَة الحلْقة؟ حاسِسْها مِش مظْبوطة.
أ: لا زيّ الفُلّ، حِلْوَة أوي!

A: Nice haircut, Darsh.
B: May God give you heaven. Is it a nice cut? I feel like it's not even.
A: No, it's perfect. Very nice!

زيّ الفُلّ [lit. like a jasmine flower] lovely, in perfect condition

You can say نَعيماً to a man or woman who has just taken a shower.

(mother to her daughter)

أ: إنْتي خدْتي دُشّ؟
ب: آه يا ماما.
أ: نَعيماً.

A: Did you take a shower?
B: Yes, Mom.
A: Heavenly!

مَعْقُول

reasonable

When used simply as an adjective, مَعْقُول **means** reasonable.

أ: أظُنّ لَوْ عمِلْنا الفرح بعْد العيد هَيِبْقى مُناسِب، مِش كِده؟

ب: آه كِده معْقول جِدّاً.

A: I think if we have the wedding after the holiday, it will be convenient, right?
B: Yeah, that's very reasonable.

أ: البِلوزة دي عجبِتْني و سِعْرها ٣٥٠. تِفْتِكري غالْيَة؟

ب: لا سِعْرها معْقول. حِلْوَة أوي فِعْلاً.

A: I like this blouse, and it costs 350 [LE]. Do you think it's expensive?
B: No, that's reasonable (affordable). It's really quite nice!

أ: أيْه رأيِك في الكلام اللي بِتْقولُه أُخْتِك ده؟
ب: واللهِ يا ماما، أنا شايْفاه كلام معْقول.

A: What do you think about what your sister said?
B: Honestly, Mom, I think it's fine.

However, معْقول is also used as an exclamation to express amazement and disbelief.

أ: سِمِعْت إنّهُم مِسْكوا مُحافِظ الجِيزة بِتُهْمِة الرِّشْوَة.
ب: معْقول؟! ده راجِل مُحْترم.

A: I heard they arrested the governor of Giza for bribery.
B: Is it possible?! That man is respectable.

أ: معْقول يعْمِل فيّا كِده بعْد كُلّ اللي عمِلْتُه عشانُه؟
ب: متِسْتغْرِبيش النُّفوس بِتِتْغيّر.

A: Unbelievable that he's doing this to me after all I've done for him!
B: Don't be surprised that people's characters change.

The synonymous exclamation معْقولة (دي) is feminine because it refers to an implied (but unexpressed) feminine noun such as حِكايَة or قِصّة.

أ: تخيّلي سعيد بعْد كُلّ ده قرّر يِهاجِر!
ب: معْقولة دي؟! ده كان ضِدّ الهِجْرة طول عُمْرُه.

A: Can you imagine, after everything, Saeed has decided to emigrate.
B: What? How can that be? He has always been against emigration.

مِش مَعْقول expresses an even stronger sense of amazement (or disbelief): No way!

أ: إمْبارِح أوِّل ما وَصلْت الشُّغْل لقيْت مُديري عايِزْني و قرَّر يِدّيني مُكافْأة.

ب: مِش مَعْقول! طب حِلْو جِدّاً!

A: Yesterday, as soon as I arrived at work, my boss wanted to see me and decided to give me a bonus.
B: No way! That's awesome!

عشم

hope and faith

The noun عشم is often translated as expectation or hope, but something is lost in translation there. عشم is a popular concept in Egyptian culture and means the kind of hope, trust, or faith that someone puts in someone they appreciate or are close to, essentially combining expectation and hope. It is used in some common set expressions:

ده العشم expresses confidence in someone: I'm counting on you. It subtly lets them know that you are counting on them not to let you down.

أ: متقلْقِش يابْني، إن شاء الله أوّل ما تِحْجِز التّذْكرة و تبلّغْني. هكون مِسْتنّيك في المطار.

ب: ده العشم يا حبيبي.

A: Don't worry, man. God willing, once you book your flight ticket, let me know, and I'll be waiting for you at the airport.
B: I'd expect nothing less from you, dear.

أ: بقولَّك أيْه! قوليلي هتِنْقِلوا إمْتى بِالظّبْط عشان أبْقى معاكي.

ب: تِسْلمي يا حبيبْتي. ده العشم.

A: Hey! Let me know exactly when you'll be moving so that I can be there [to help].
B: Bless you, dear. I know I can count on you.

The opposite expression is مكانْش العشم **implies disappointment, that I wouldn't have expected this from you.**

أ: معلِشّ سامِحْني مقدِرْتِش آجي إمْبارِح.

ب: مكانْش العشم يا صاحْبي. كِده تْسيبْني في يوْم زيّ ده؟

A: I'm sorry. Forgive me, I couldn't come yesterday
B: I was counting on you, buddy. How could you leave me hanging on such a day?

The expression عشمي في ربِّنا كِبير 'my faith in God is great' **expresses optimism.**

أ: إنْتَ مْصدّق إنّ إبْنك مُمْكِن يِظْهر تاني بعْد العُمْر ده كُلُّه؟

ب: عشمي في ربِّنا كِبير.

A: Do you believe that your son will appear again after all these years?
B: My faith in God is great.

أ: أنا عِشمي كِبير في ربّنا إنّ السّنة اللي جايّة المبيعات هتِعْلى.
ب: إن شاء الله. يا مُسهِّل!

A: My faith in God is great that next year sales will increase.
B: God willing. Let's see!

يا مُسهِّل [lit. o he who facilitates] is an invocation of God.

The expression مكانش العشم [lit. this wasn't the hope] assigns blame and shows disappointment when someone has let you down and not lived up to expectations.

أ: مكانش العشم يا حُسام بعْد كلّ العِشْرة دي متْجيش تعزّيني في أبويا.
ب: والله يا مْحمّد، أنا عارف إنّي أسْتاهِل أيّ عِتاب منّك بسّ حقيقي كُنْت مطْحون في الشُّغْل.

A: This wasn't what I expected from you, Hossam, after all these years, that you wouldn't offer me condolences upon my father's death.
B: Seriously, Mohamed, I know I deserve any blame from your end, but I've really been crushed at work.

The expression عشم إبْليس في الجنّة [lit. Satan's hope for Paradise] implies that something is impossible–as impossible as Satan entering Paradise–and discourages futile hope.

أ: أنا عنْدي أمل كِبير إنّ بيت الدّرْب الأصْفر يِتْباع و يفُكّ الزّنْقة اللي إحْنا فيها.

ب: عشم إبْليس في الجنّة! إنْتَ عارِف البيْت ده بقالُه كام سنة؟ مين مُمْكِن يِفكّر يِشْتِريه!

A: I have high hopes that the house in El-Darb El-Asfar will get sold and alleviate the financial strain we are in.
B: That's like Satan's hope for Heaven! Do you have any idea how [many years] old this building is? Who would ever think to buy it!

أ: محْمود فاكِر إنُّه هُوَّ اللي هَياخُد منْصِب المُدير الجِديد.

ب: ده عشم إبْليس في الجنّة! ده آخِر واحِد مُمْكِن ياخُد ترْقِية... على جُثّتي! تقاريرُه كُلّها زيّ الزِّفْت.

A: Mahmoud believes he'll be getting the new managerial post.
B: When pigs fly! He's the last person that could get a promotion... over my dead body. All of his reports are horrible.

The concept of عشم **can be expressed by the adjective** عشْمان: hopeful, expectant.

أ: أنا عشْمانة السِّكّة النّهارْده تِكون فاضْيَة، مِش زيّ إمْبارِح.

ب: و مين سِمِعك! ده الواحِد إمْبارِح وَصل بيْتُه بِطْلوع الرّوح.

A: I'm hopeful that traffic today will be light, unlike yesterday.
B: Tell me about it! People have barely gotten home from yesterday.

The idiom بِطْلوع الرّوح [lit. with the release of the soul (upon dying)] means barely.

أ: يافندم، أنا جايْلك و عشْمان في كرمك.
ب: يابني، اِعْتِبـر المَوْضوع خلْصان.

A: Sir, I'm coming to you full of faith in your generosity.
B: My son, consider it done.

The concept of having عشم can be expressed by the synonymous intransitive verbs عِشِم and اِتْعَشِّم.

أ: إن شاء الله عمّو وَعدْني يِشغّلْني معاه في الصَّيْدلية أوِّل ما أتْخرّج.
ب: متِتْعشّمْش أوي كِده... عشان هُوَّ أصلاً اِحْتِمال يِبيعْها و يِسيب البلد.

A: God willing, Uncle promised me he will hire me at his pharmacy once I graduate.
B: Don't put that much expectation and faith in it... because he could sell it and leave the country.

أ: تِفْتِكِري ماجِد هَيقْدر يجيب الحاجات اللي طلبْناها مِنُّه قبْل ما يِنْزِل مصْر؟
ب: أنا حاسّة إنّنا عشمْنا بِزِيادة.
أ: طيّب نِكلّمُه نقولُّه إنُّه لَوْ قِدِر علشان مَيِضْغطْش على نفْسُه.

A: Do you think Maged will be able to bring the stuff we requested from him when he comes back to Egypt?
B: I feel like maybe we asked too much of him.
A: Then we should call him and tell him 'only if' he can and not to trouble himself.

The transitive verb عشّم **means to cause someone to have expectations of you by overpromising something you cannot deliver:** to raise someone's hopes

أ: شُفْتي سْليم عمل فيّا أيْه! فضِل يِعشِّمْني إنُّه عنْدُه شقّة في السُّويْس مُمْكِن أنْزِل فيها و لمّا رُحْت لقيْتُه مأجِّرْها!

ب: آدي آخْرِةْ العشم. قُلْتِلك متِعْتِمِدْش عليْه و اعْمِل حِسابك على مكان تاني.

A: Did you see what Selim did to me! He kept assuring me that he has an apartment in Suez that I can stay in, and when I went, I found out he's renting it out!
B: That's what happens with hope and expectation! I told you not to count on him and to have a backup plan for another place.

Section 2
Being Negative

In section 2, we learn more, essential, everyday expressions and adverbs–but these all have negative connotations.

track 014	page 58	Enough!	بسّ
track 015	page 60	Never mind!	معلِشّ
track 016	page 65	No way!	اِبْقى قابِلْني
track 017	page 67	No can do!	مَينفعْش
track 018	page 69	"without anything"	بلاش
track 019	page 73	nonsense	أيّ كلام
track 020	page 76	unacceptable	عيْب
track 021	page 80	forbidden	حرام
track 022	page 85	corrupt	شِمال
track 023	page 88	not in a million years	في المِشْمِش
track 024	page 89	Oh, my Joy!	يا فرْحِتي

بسّ

Enough!

You're likely aware that بسّ is used as the conjunction **but** and the adverb **only/just**. **But it is also used as an exclamation (often followed by بقى):** Stop it! / Enough already! / Knock it off!

أ: ماما! آدم أخد اللِّعْبة مِنّي.
ب: هُوَّ اللي أخدْها مِنّي الأوِّل.
أ: بسّ بقى! صدَّعْتوني... لا إنْتَ وَلا هُوَّ! هاتوا اللِّعْبة.

A: Mom, Adam took the toy from me.
B: He took it first!
A: Enough already! You've given me a headache. Neither one of you [gets it]. Bring me the toy.

بسّ **can be emphasized by elongating the vowel or repeating it.**

أ: شُفْتي حصل أيه إمْبارِحْ؟ أوِّل ما رِجِعْت مِن الفرح لقيْت عمَّتي مْكلِّماني...

ب: بااااسّ! بِالرّاحة يا بِنْتي! طب قولي صَباح الخير الأوّل! فَرح مين أصْلاً؟

A: Know what happened yesterday? As soon as I got back from the wedding, my aunt called me...
B: Hold up! Calm down, girl! Say good morning first! Whose wedding now?

Less dramatically, بسّ can signal that something is sufficient.

أ: تِحِبّ أحُطّلك نِعْناع على الشّاي؟
ب: آه يا ريْت... تِسْلم إيدك. بسّ... كِفايَة كِده. حِلْو أوي!

A: Would you like me to add mint to the tea for you?
B: Yes, please... bless you. Okay, that's enough. Perfect!

At the end of a statement, و بسّ (كده) means 'And that's all/it!', 'And no more.'

أ: تِفْتِكِر أعْمِل تحْليل للنّتايج وَلّا كِفايَة أرْصُدها بسّ؟
ب: لا، أرْصُد كلّ النّتايج في جدْوَل و رتِّبْهُم و بسّ.

A: Do you think I should make an analysis of the results, or would it be enough just to track them?
B: Just track all the results, organize them, and that's it.

أ: هُوَّ فيه حاجة بعْمِلها بعْد ما بدخّلْها الفُرْن؟
ب: لا بتْحُطّي الموتْزاريلّا على الوِشّ و تدخّليها الفُرْن و بسّ كِده.

A: Is there anything else I should do after I put it in the oven?
B: No, you add the mozzarella on top, put it in the oven, and that's it.

معلِشّ

Never mind!

معلِشّ is used to downplay a situation, whether to console, sympathize, or apologize. The word originally comes from the Modern Standard Arabic phrase ما عليه شيء, which literally means nothing against it.

معلِشّ can express sympathy.

أ: تخيّل بعْد كلّ الشُّغْل ده رفدوني.
ب: معلِشّ هوِّن على نفْسك. إن شاء الله ربّنا يِعوّضك بِشُغْل أحْسن.

A: Imagine! After all this work, they fired me.
B: It's okay. Take it easy. God willing, our Lord will compensate you with a better job.

أ: أنا تعْبانة أوي، مِش عارْفة أركِّز في المُذاكْرة.
ب: معلِشّ يا حبيبتي، ادْخُلي ريّحي ساعة و قومي كمِّلي.

A: I'm so tired I can't concentrate on studying.
B: Don't be upset, dear. Relax for an hour and then resume [studying].

أ: النّهارْده عربية خبطِت فيّا، وَقَّعِتْلي الإكْصِدام
ب: معلِشّ، جت سليمة. المهمّ إنّك بِخيْر.

A: Today a car crashed into mine, and made my bumper fall off.
B: Never mind. It's a minor thing. What's important is that you're okay.

جت سليمة is interchangeable with حصل خير. Both mean it turned out soundly and are used to assure someone that an incident was minor and could have been worse.

أ: ماما، أنا رجّعْت النّهارْده في المدرسة...
ب: معلِشّ يا حبيبي. ألف سلامة عليْك. حاوِل تِنْزِل بُكْره على مِعْدة خفيفة.

A: Mom, today I threw up at school...
B: Oh! It's okay, sweetie. I hope you feel better. Just try tomorrow to leave with a light stomach [that is, not eat too much].

أ: شُفْتي إزّاي عدِّت وَلا كإنّها شايْفاني.
ب: معلِشّ، تِلاقيها مِش واخْدة بالْها.

A: Look how she walked by as if she didn't see me!
B: Don't worry. Maybe she didn't notice [you].

معلشّ is sometimes used to ask for a favor, as a sort of apology for the imposition.

أ: معلشّ مُمْكِن أعدّي؟
ب: آه طبْعاً، اتْفضّلي.

A: Excuse me, can I just get past?
B: Oh, sure! Please!

(to a taxi driver)

أ: معلشّ مُمْكِن نُقِف هِنا دِقيقة أشْتِري حاجة بسُرْعة؟
ب: طبْعاً يافنْدِم. خُدي وقْتِك.

A: Excuse me, could we stop here for a minute (so that) I would buy something quickly
B: Of course, ma'am. Take your time.

(between two coworkers)

أ: معلشّ لوْ ينْفع نِبدّل أجازِتْنا الأسْبوع الجايّ؟
ب: مفيش مُشْكِلة. قولّي تِحِبّ نظبّطْها إزّاي.

A: Sorry to bother, but could we switch days off next week?
B: No problem. Tell me how you would like us to arrange it.

أ: معلشّ هتْعِبك بسّ مُمْكِن تِجيبْلي كوبّايةْ مايّة؟
ب: طبْعاً يا عمّو! ثواني تِكون عنْدك.

A: Sorry to bother, but could you please bring me a glass of water?
B: Of course, uncle! Just a moment, and you'll have it.

معلِشّ is used as an apology for an unintentional inconvenience, especially when bumping into someone or stepping on their foot.

أ: ما تْفتّح يا عمرّ!
ب: معلِشّ.
أ: معلِشّ دي أصرِفْها مْنين؟
ب: ما خلاصّ! قُلْنا معلِشّ يا عمرّ!

A: Hey, watch out! Are you blind?!
B: Sorry.
A: What will I gain from your 'sorry'?
B: Enough! I said sorry, man!

أ: أيْه اللي إنْتَ عمِلتُه ده؟ كسرْتها!
ب: معلِشّ حقّك عليّا. هجيبْلك غيرْها.

A: What have you done?! You broke it!
B: Sorry, it's my mistake. I'll get you another one.

Often preceded by لا and spoken with a serious or angry tone, معلِشّ is used to correct someone and absolve oneself from responsibility–that is, to set the record straight.

أ: حضْرِتك طلبْت منْدوب يِيجيلك بُكْره خمْسة العصْر؟
ب: لأ معلِشّ، ثانْيَة واحْدة. أنا اتّصلْت إمْبارِح و بلّغْتُكُم إنّي لغيْت المعاد.

A: You requested a representative to come to you tomorrow at 5 p.m., right?
B: No, excuse me, hold on a second! I called yesterday and canceled the appointment.

أ: خلاص لَوْ كِده هنِضْطرّ نِرْجع على مصْر.
ب: لا معلِشّ، ده مكانْش اتِّفاقْنا. إحْنا قُلْنا هنِرْجع لمّا الأَوْلاد يِدْخُلوا كُلِّية.

A: Well, that's that. In that case, we'll have to return to Egypt.
B: No, excuse me, but that was not our agreement. We agreed that we would go back when the kids go to college.

اِبْقى قابِلْني

No way!

اِبْقى قابِلْني [lit. then meet me] indicates that you think that something is extremely unlikely to happen. It means 'Do find me,' as in 'Do come find me if I'm wrong about this and make me eat my words.' The expression is an imperative, so it varies in gender and number according to the addressee.

m.	اِبْقى قابِلْني
f.	اِبْقي قابِليني
pl.	اِبْقوا قابِلوني

أ: إن شاء الله تتْخرّج إنْتَ بسّ و تْلاقي شُغْلانة مُحْترمة بِمرتّب معْقول تِقْدر تِجيب منهُ شقّة.

ب: اِبْقى قابِلْني! هُوَّ فيه مرتّب بيْكفّي مُواصَلات و أكْل حتّى علشان أجيب مِنهُ شقّة!

A: God willing, you will graduate and find a decent job with a reasonable salary from which you can save up to buy an apartment.

B: Fat chance! Is there even a salary that covers transportation and food, let alone [enough] to buy an apartment!

أ: أنا واثْقة إنُّه هَيِتْغيّر و يْبطّل سجايِر على إيدي.
ب: هاها، اِبْقي قابْليني. يا بِنْتي السّجايِر دي إدْمان أصْعب مِن المُخدّرات!

A: I'm sure he'll change and quit smoking with my help.
B: Haha! There's no way in hell! Girl, smoking is a stronger addiction than drugs.

أ: إحْنا قرّرْنا نِطْلع السّنة دي مِن الأوائِل.
ب: اِبْقوا قابْلوني!

A: We've decided to get the best grades in class this year.
B: In your dreams!

The expression can be followed by لَوْ and the unlikely event with a perfect-tense verb.

اِبْقى قابِلْني لَوْ وِصِلْنا في معادْنا!

There's no way we'll arrive on time!

There is also a synonymous expression, آدي دقْني, which literally means 'Here is my chin.'

آدي دقْني لَوْ فلحْتوا السّنة دي.

No way you'll get good grades this year!

مَيْنفَعْش

No can do!

The verb نفع **means** to work (out), to be of use. **The negative third-person masculine singular form** مَيْنفَعْش **is** used in some idiomatic constructions to imply that something is impossible.

present	مَيْنفَعْش
past	مكانْش يِنْفَع
future	مِش هَيِنْفَع

أ: ماما، عايِز شوكولاتة!
ب: مَيْنفَعْش يا حبيبي دِلْوَقْتي. إحْنا هنِتْغدّى.

A: Mom, I want some chocolate!
B: Not now, honey. We're going to have lunch.

أ: كُنْتي رْكِبْتي معاهُم و وَصَلّوكي بالمرّة.
ب: مكانْش يِنْفَع. العربية كانِت على آخِرْها.

A: You should have gotten a ride with them so that they could drop you off on their way.
B: There was no way. The car was full up [with passengers].

Preceding a bare imperfect verb in a question, it is used to make a request by asking whether something is possible.

أ: مَيِنْفعْش تْجيبيلي معاكي المخدّة مِن جُوّه؟ أنا مْكسِّلة أقوم.

ب: حاضِر!

A: Won't [lit. is it not possible that] you bring me the pillow from inside? I'm too lazy to get up.
B: All right.

(A client speaking to an interior designer.)

أ: مَيِنْفعْش يا باشْمُهنْدِس نِغيّر اللّوْن ده؟

ب: طبْعاً ينْفع بسّ كِده مِش هَيِبْقى ماشي مع باقي الشّقّة.

A: Can't we change this color, architect?
B: Sure we can, but then it won't match with the rest of the apartment.

The client addresses the interior designer with the respectful title for that profession: باشْمُهنْدِس (See p. 112)

بلاش

"without anything"

The word بلاش originally comes from the Modern Standard Arabic بلا شيء, which literally means without anything.

When followed by a noun, بلاش (or ما بلاش) is used to recommend against that thing or person.

أ: آخُد الشَّنْطة الحمْرا وَلّا السّوْدا؟
ب: لأ بلاش الحمْرا. خُدي السّوْدا.

A: Shall I get the red purse or the black one?
B: Forget the red one. Buy the black one.

أ: أنا هروح القاهِرة بِالعربية.
ب: لا بلاش العربية. روحي بِالقطْر أحْسن.

A: I'll take the car to Cairo.
B: Forget the car. You'd best take the train.

أ: أنا هَعْمِل العملية مع الدُّكْتور اللي رُحْناله.
ب: ما بلاش الدُّكْتور ده! أنا مرْتحْتُلوش خالِص.

A: I'll get the surgery with the doctor we visited.
B: I'd advise against that doctor! I didn't feel comfortable around him at all.

بلاش can also be followed by an imperfect verb. It is softer than a negative command.

أ: هطلّع الشّهادة يوْم الاتْنيْن إن شاء الله.
ب: بلاش تِروح يوْم الاتْنيْن. هَيِبْقى زحْمة.

A: I'm going to go get the certificate on Monday, God willing.
B: You'd best not go on Monday. It will be crowded.

بلاش is also used to tell someone to stop doing something that they have already started.

أ: إنْتَ بْتِعْمِل أيْه؟
ب: بحاوِل أصلّح المرْوَحة.
أ: طبّ بسّ بلاش تِفُكّها كِده و خلّينا نْودّيها التَّوكيل.

A: What are you doing?
B: I'm trying to fix the fan.
A: Wait! Stop disassembling it like that. Let's take it to the service center.

بلاش and ما بلاش can be used elliptically (that is, in isolation, with an unexpressed noun or verb, when it is understood from the context).

أ: أنا خلاص قرّرْت أسْتقيل الشّهْر اللي جايّ.
ب: ما بلاش! اُصْبرُ لمّا تْلاقي شُغْل تاني أحْسن.

A: That's it! I've decided to quit my job next month.
B: No, don't! Be patient until you find a better job.

Only related in meaning to the above uses when you consider the original meaning ('without anything'), يا بلاش is an exclamatory response: How cheap!

أ: معْروض عليّا العربية دي كسْر زيرو بتمانين ألْف.
ب: يا بلاش! دي الجْديدة مِنْها تِعدّي المية و عِشْرين.

A: Someone is offering me a 'newly used' model of this car for 80,000 [pounds].
B: How cheap! The new one is more than 120 [thousand].

أ: جِبْتي الشّنْطة دي بْكام؟
ب: مش هتْصدّقي، جِبْتها من ع الرّصيف بخمْسين جِنيْه بسّ.
أ: يا بلاش والله!

A: How much did you get this purse for?
B: You won't believe it. I got it from a street vendor for just 50 pounds.
A: Wow! That's so cheap!

بِبلاش is used adverbially to mean for free.

أ: اللّه! أيْه السّلْسِلة الجميلة دي! جِبْتيها مْنيْن و بْكام؟
ب: أخدْتها ببلاش هِدية على شنْطة في أوكازيوْن.

71 | TALK LIKE AN EGYPTIAN

A: Wow! What a beautiful necklace! Where did you get it? And for how much?
B: I got it for free as a gift for buying a purse on a sale.

أ: بِكام دي لَوْ سمحْت؟
ب: بِلاش يافنْدِم. دي عيّنات مجّانية.

A: How much is this, please?
B: It's free, ma'am. They're free samples.

Although the samples actually are free in the above example, keep in mind, when it comes time to pay and you inquire about the total, that it is common in Egypt for the salesperson (server, taxi driver, etc.) to reply, at first, that it is "free." But this is an expression of hospitality not to be taken literally. They do expect you to pay!

أ: بِكام الطّرْحة دي مِن فضْلِك؟
ب: بِلاش عشان خاطْرِك.
أ: تِسْلمي! عايْزة أعْرف سِعْرها بْجدّ.
ب: بِسبْعين بسّ لَوْ أخدْتي اتنيْن فيه عرْض تاخْدي التّالْتة بِلاش.

A: How much is this headscarf?
B: For you, it's free!
A: Thank you... but I really want to know its price.
B: It's 70 [pounds], but if you buy two, there's an offer where you can take the third for free.

أيّ كلام

nonsense

أيّ كلام [lit. any talk] means nonsense, implying that something is a joke or worthless.

أ: للأسف ملْحقْتش اجْتِماع النّهارْده. فاتْني كتير؟
ب: لأ خالِص. الاجْتِماع أيّ كلام و مكانْش فيه أيّ جْديد.

A: Unfortunately, I couldn't make today's meeting. Did I miss a lot?
B: Not at all. The meeting was a joke. There was nothing new.

أ: شفْت إبْراهيم إمْبارِح كان بيْقولّي أيْه؟
ب: يا راجِل، سيبك مِنُّه. ده بيْقول أيّ كلام.
أ: بالعكْس، أنا حاسِس إنُّه كلامُه كلُّه كان واقِعي جِدّاً.

A: Did you hear what Ibrahim was saying to me yesterday?
B: Oh man, forget about him. He just talks nonsense.
A: Contrary! I feel that everything he said was so true.

أيّ كلام can also describe something of low quality or that does **not work well**: shoddy, flimsy, iffy.

أ: أحُطّ الكَرْتونة فيْن؟ على التَّرابيْزة دي؟

ب: لا لا دي ترابيْزة أيّ كلام متِسْتحْمِلْش الكَرْتونة التِّقيلة دي.

A: Where shall I put the box? On that table?
B: No, no! That's a flimsy table that wouldn't support such a heavy box.

أ: أخْبار الموبايْل الجِديد أيْه؟

ب: اِسْكُتي! مِش طِلِع أيّ كلام و شكْلي اتْضحك عليّا.

A: How's the new cell phone?
B: Don't ask! It turned out to be a real lemon. It seems I got conned.

While اِسْكُت means *shut up*, followed by مِش..., it forms an expression meaning *don't ask!* (Notice that مش is not making the following sentence logically negative, which would be مطِلعْش.)

أيّ كلام can also be used adverbially to mean *any old way* or *carelessly*.

أ: عايِزْني أحُطّ الكُتُب إزّاي في المكْتبة؟

ب: حُطّيهُم بسّ دِلْوَقْتي أيّ كلام... و أنا أبْقى أروّقْهُم بعْدين.

A: How would you like me to put the books on the shelf?
B: Put them any old way for now. I'll organize them later.

أ: صلّحْتوا باب الشّقّة؟
ب: آه جِبْنا نجّار بسّ صلّحُه أيّ كلام. هنْجيب واحِد تاني يُظْبُط الشُّغْل.

A: Did you get the front door repaired?
B: Yes, we brought in a carpenter, but he fixed it carelessly. We'll bring another one to fix his work.

أ: متِعْرفيش واحْدة سِتّ تيجي تِنضّفْلي البيْت كُلّ جُمْعة؟
ب: أعْرف واحْدة بسّ بِتْنضّف أيّ كلام. مِش هتريّحِك يَعْني.

A: Don't you know a woman who could come over to clean the house every Friday?
B: I know one, but she cleans carelessly... You wouldn't be happy with her.

عيْب

unacceptable

In Modern Standard Arabic, عيْب can mean flaw (in manufacturing). But in Egyptian Arabic, عيْب more commonly refers to inappropriate or even shameful behavior.

عيْب expresses that you find something unacceptable, whether you are reprimanding, reminding, or just commenting on someone's behavior or words.

أ: ماما، محمّد قالّي إنّه عمّو سعيد غِلِس أوي.
ب: عيْب يا وَلد نِتكلّم على حد كبير كِده.

A: Mom, Mohamed told me that Uncle Saeed is a pain in the butt.
B: It's not right to talk about an adult that way, boy.

أ: تِفتِكري تِبقى قِلّة ذوْق لوْ ما عزمْتِش طنْط سنيّة؟
ب: لا عيْب برْضُه! السِّت ياما عزمِتنا في مُناسبات.

A: Do you think it would be bad manners if I didn't invite Auntie Saneyya?

B: That'd be absolutely unacceptable! The woman has always invited us over on special occasions.

أ: شايْفة الرّاجِل بِيْسوق إزّاي! وَلا مِحْتِرِم إشارة وَلا سُرْعة.

ب: والله عِيْب كِده! النّاس دي بِتاخُد رُخَص إزّاي!

A: See how that man drives! No respect for traffic lights or the speed limit.
B: So shameful! How do these people get driver's licenses?

عِيْب is also used more playfully to assure someone that they are welcome to take or do something (as in 'shame on you for even asking'), or to feign insult that they would even ask–as a modest brag.

أ: رنا، مُمْكِن تِسلِّفيني الشَّنْطة البُنّي بْتاعْتِك النّهارْده بَسّ؟

ب: عِيْب يا بِنْتي! خُديها أيّ وَقْت!

A: Rana, could you please lend me your brown bag just for today?
B: Come on! Don't even ask, girl! Take it any time!

أ: اِوْعى تْكون لِسّا مبعتّش السّي ڤي!

ب: عِيْب و دي تْفوتْني برْضُه؟ بعَتّ مِن أُسْبوعيْن.

A: Don't tell me you haven't sent your CV yet!
B: Uh! Come on! Would I miss such a thing? I sent it two weeks ago.

أ: عملْت أيْه في المُقابلة؟ طمِّنّي!

ب: عيْب عليْك! عايْزيني أبْتِدي مِن بُكْره.

A: How did you do in the interview? Tell me!
B: Shame on you even needing to ask! They want me to start tomorrow.

العيْب عليْه **means** one is to blame; it's one's fault; shame on one.

أ: تخيَّل مُراد بعْد السِّنين دي كُلّها مرضاش يِقسِّم التِّركة.

ب: العيْب مِش عليْه. العيْب على اللي سابُه السنين دي كُلّها يِتْحكَّم في المَوْضوع.

A: (Can you) imagine! Murad, after all these years, refused to distribute the inheritance
B: The blame is not on him. It's on whoever left him in control of everything all these years.

أ: شُفْت عملوا أيْه معايا بعْد كُلّ الشُّغْل ده؟

ب: عايِز الحقّ؟ العيْب مِش عليْهُم. العيْب عليْك إنْتَ علشان اِتْنازلْت عن حُقوقك طول السِّنين دي.

A: Did you see what they did to me after all that work?!
B: You want the truth? The blame is not theirs... It's yours because you gave up your rights over the years.

أ: إنْتَ أيْه رأيُك في مَوْقِف رانْيا إمْبارِح؟
ب: العيْب عليْها. طبْعاً مكانْش يِصِحّ تِغْلِط في صلاح قُدّامْنا. بِصراحة الغلط راكِبْها مِن ساسْها لِراسْها.
أ: أنا معاك بسّ أكيد مفيش دُخان مِن غيْر نار.

A: What do you think about Rania's attitude yesterday?
B: She was in the wrong. It wasn't appropriate at all to humiliate Salah in front of us. Honestly, she's completely to blame.
A: I agree with you... but there's no smoke without fire.

مِن ساسُه لِراسُه *from head to toe, completely*

مفيش دُخان مِن غيْر نار [lit. *there's no smoke without fire*] means that it's not out of the blue—there must be an underlying cause

حرام

forbidden

Things that are forbidden according to Islam are حرام.

أ: إنْتَ متعرفْش إنّ الخمْرة حرام؟
ب: أنا هدوق بسّ، ده بُقّ واحِد.
أ: حتّى لَو نُقطة برضُه حرام طالما الكِتير مِنُّه هَيْخَلِّيك تِسْكر.

A: Don't you know that alcohol is forbidden [in Islam]?
B: I'll just have a taste. It's only one sip.
A: Even if it's one drop, it's still forbidden as long as plenty would get you drunk.

أ: هِيَّ الفَوايد الثّابْتة حلال وَلّا حرام؟
ب: حرام طبْعاً عشان بتِبْقى زيّ الرِّبا.

A: Are fixed interest rates permitted or forbidden [in Islam]?
B: Of course, forbidden, since it's just like usury.

حرام is also used (as an invariable adjective) in a less religious sense to refer more broadly to something that is morally (and likely legally) objectionable: dirty, shady, sinful. (See also p. 85.)

أ: إنْتَ لِيْه مبعْتِش المحلّ لِوْلاد زكي؟
ب: يابْني، دوْل ناس شُغْلُهُم حرام. أبيعْلُهُم أنا المحلّ يعْمِلوا شُغْلُهُم فيه؟!

A: Why didn't you sell the shop to Zaki's sons?
B: Man, these people are involved in some shady business. Was I to sell the shop to them so they can do their business in it?!

أ: فِلوس الصّفْقة دي لازِم نقسِّمْها عليْنا بِالعدْل.
ب: أنا مِش هاخُد ولا مِلّيم. دي فِلوس حرام أصْلاً.

A: This money from this deal has to be divided among us fairly.
B: I won't take a penny. This is dirty money to begin with!

أ: أنا مِش عارِف النّاس دي بتْنام على المخدّة إزّاي!
ب: النّاس دي عيشِتْهُم حرام في حرام. عايْشين بِالطّول و العرْض و مِش عامْلين حِساب لِلآخْرة.

A: I don't know how these people can sleep at night!
B: Their way of life is full of sin. They live excessively to the maximum and never prepare for the afterlife.

Notice the emphasized expression حرام في حرام *sin upon sin*.

إبْن حرام (plural: وْلاد حرام) originally meant bastard, in the literal sense of being born illegitimately (outside of wedlock); however, nowadays it is only used as an insult.

أ: مِش مُمْكِن! مِش عارِف أخلّص حاجة مِن غيْر ما أدْفع رِشْوَة!

ب: ولاد الحرام، مسابوش لِولاد الحلال حاجة.

A: This is impossible! I can't get anything done without paying a bribe!
B: Bastards have left nothing for the legitimate.

This is an idiom meaning that evil has left no room for good.

Its opposite, إبْن حلال (literally, someone born legitimately) describes a kind and decent person.

أ: بسّ تْصدّق مُعِزّ ده طِلع إبْن حلال.

ب: إبْن حلال مين يابْني! ده عيِّل إبْن حرام. كُلّ شُغْلُه شِمال.

A: You know, Moez really turned out to be quite a decent guy.
B: Decent guy?! Who?! He's a real bastard. Everything he does is shady.

In addition to its original meaning as forbidden, حرام can also describe something that you find unacceptable, unfair, or inappropriate.

أ: شُفْت اللي حصل مع محْمود إمْبارِح؟
ب: بِجدّ حرام أوي اللى حصل ده. مكانْش يِسْتاهِل الرفْد. المَوْضوع كِبِر أوي و حاسِس إنُّه ظُلْم كبير ليه.

A: Did you see what happened with Mahmoud yesterday?
B: Seriously, what happened is totally unfair. He didn't deserve to be fired. The issue got blown out of proportion, and I feel it's such an injustice for him.

أ: شُفْتي الأخْبار؟
ب: حاجة مُحْزِنة! والله اللي بيِحْصل ده حرام.

A: Did you see the news?
B: It's so depressing. What's happening is really unacceptable.

يا حرام is an exclamation that expresses sympathy for someone in an unfair or unacceptable situation.

أ: الواد يا عيْني كان نايِم في الأرْض مِن غيرْ غطا.
ب: يا حرام!

A: Poor boy! He was sleeping on the floor without a cover.
B: Oh my!

أ: شُفْتي الحادْثة كْبيرة إزّاي!
ب: يا حرام! العربية اتْدمرِت. أكيد اللي جُوّه اتْبهْدِل. ربِّنا يُسْتر.

A: Look how big the accident is!
B: Oh no! The car is damaged. I'm sure the person inside has been injured. God help [them]!

حرام عليْه shame on one **is used to scold or rebuke someone whose behavior is unacceptable.**

أ: جيرانّا اللي فوْق حابْسين قُطّة و مْسافْرين.
ب: حرام عليْهُم بِجدّ! إزّاي يعْمِلوا كِده!

A: Our neighbors upstairs have locked in their cat while they're away.
B: Shame on them, seriously! How could they do such a thing!

أ: أنا بفكّر أطلّق مِراتي و أسافِر أعيش حَياتي.
ب: حرام عليْك يا أخي بقى بعْد كُلّ العِشْرة دي تِسيبْها و تْشوف نفْسك.

A: I'm thinking about divorcing my wife and traveling to start over.
B: Shame on you, man! After all these years, you'd leave her and only look after yourself?

(The second speaker feels her rights have been violated.)

أ: المَوْضوع اِنْتهى خلاص!
ب: اِنْتهى إزّاي؟! و حقّي أجيبُه مْنيْن؟ حرام عليْكو!

A: Well, that's the end of the matter!
B: The end? And how do I regain my rights? Shame on you!

شِمال

corrupt

The original meaning of the invariable adjective شِمال is left (not to be confused with شَمال north), but a more recent colloquial meaning has emerged with a negative connotation in reference to one's character, morals, or actions: corrupt, dirty, debaucherous, promiscuous, etc.

أ: سِمِعْت عن مُحامي إسْمُه صادِق بشير؟
ب: اِوْعى تْروحْله، ده مُحامي شِمال و سُمْعِتُه زيّ الزِّفْت.

A: Have you ever heard of a lawyer named Sadeq Besheer?
B: Don't you ever go to him! He's a dirty/corrupt lawyer, and his reputation is awful.

أ: بقولّك أيْه! سعيد عازِمْنا الخميس اللي جايّ على حفْلة عنْدُه في البيْت.
ب: بلاش أحْسن. سعيد ده كُلّ قعْداتُه شْمال.

A: You know what! Saeed is inviting us to a party at his place next Thursday.
B: We'd best not [go]. Saeed's gatherings are all debaucherous.

It can be used in the context of one's chastity, implying inappropriate behavior around the opposite sex.

أ: حقيقي نَوال كُلّ شُغْلها شْمال؟
ب: دي شْمال الشِّمال يا بِنْتي! لأ، اِوْعي تِدْخُلي معاها في أيّ مَوْضوع.

A: Is it true that Nawal's a promiscuous/easy/dirty girl?
B: She's the dirtiest of the dirty, girl! Beware of having anything to do with her.

It can also refer to homosexuals—of course, with the same negative connotation.

أ: صحيح البلد اللي سافِرْتِلْها آخِر مرّة فيها ناس شِمال كِتير؟
ب: بِالهبل! أنا كُنْت بتْلخْبط بِشكْل مِش طبيعي.

A: Is it true that there are a lot of queers/ladyboys in the last country you traveled to?
B: Tons! I was unsettled [by it] to no end.

However, in the expression الحِتّة الشِّمال, the connotation is positive. Literally the left part, it implies the heart's location on the left side of the body and refers to someone beloved.

أ: شُفْت الواد عمْرو عمل أيْه في باقي العيال؟
ب: بقولّك أيْه، ده الحتّهْ الشِّمال. يِعْمِل اللي هُوَّ عايْزُهْ.
أ: أمّا نْشوف آخرهْ الدلع ده أيْه.

A: See what the little boy Amr did to the other kids?
B: Hey... this dude is the "beloved" one. Let him do whatever he wants.
A: Let's see how this spoiling will end.

أ: أنا مِش هخْرُج مع أيّ حدّ النّهارْده. عايِز أريّح.
ب: إحْنا مِش كُنّا متِّفْقين نُخْرُج باللِّيْل؟
أ: لأ يا حبيبْتي، إنْتي الحتّهْ الشِّمال. أنا قصْدي على صْحابي.

A: I'm not going out with anyone today... I need to rest.
B: Didn't we agree we'd go out this evening?
A: No, honey. You're the special one. I meant with my friends.

في المِشْمِش

not in a million years

This idiom literally means 'in an apricot' and is used to express an impossibility, indicating that something or a request is impossible.

أ: هُوَّ مفيش أمل خالِص يِشْتِغِل في الشِّرْكة دي؟
ب: في المِشْمِش! دي شِرْكة صَعْبة جِدّاً و مِش بِيْعَيِّنوا غيْر مِن قرايبْهِم.

A: Is there no hope at all that he could work in this company?
B: No way! It's such a hard company [to get into] that only employs members of the family.

أ: تِفْتِكِر لَوْ اِتْقدِّمْت لِغادة، تِوافِق عليّا؟
ب: مُمْكِن آه في المِشْمِش! اِنْتو مُخْتِلفين فرْق السّما و الأرْض. مُسْتحيل المَوْضوع يِمْشي.

A: Do you think if I proposed to Ghada, she would say yes?
B: Yeah, maybe when pigs fly. You're as different as the sky and earth. There's no way that would work out.

يا فرْحِتي

Oh, my joy!

يا فرْحِتي [lit. oh, my joy] is a sarcastic response. It expresses disappointment بـ in someone or something.

أ: بسّ الشُّغْل الجِديد مُرتّبه أعْلى، مِش كِده؟
ب: يا فرْحِتي! عملْت أنا أيْه بِالمرتّب العالي و نُصُّه بيْروح المُواصلات!

A: But your new job pays more, right?
B: (sarcastically) Oh my joy! What shall I do with a high salary when half of it goes to transportation?

أ: عملْت أيْه في النّتيجة؟
ب: مقْبول الحمْدُ لِلّه!
أ: يا فرْحِتي بيك!

A: What grade did you get?
B: A 'C' [passing grade], thank God!
A: (sarcastically) I'm so proud of you!

Section 3
Addressing People

We'll start off section 3 with a formal way to address people. Then we'll look at various ways to address strangers. Next, we'll move on to people with whom you have a relationship. (When addressing someone who is not a stranger and who has certain respected occupations, you should use a specific form of address to acknowledge their professional status.) And finally, we'll examine some familial terms and how they are used with actual family members but also with non-relatives in Egyptian culture.

> When you know someone's name and are on familiar terms, of course, you can simply address that person by their name. But when the person is a stranger, or the relationship is more formal, there are special forms of address in Egyptian Arabic. Using the wrong one can be amusing at best and offensive at worst, so it's important to know when to use–and when not to use–certain terms. How you address someone depends not only on their gender, age, and social/professional status but also on yours and your relation to that person.

track 025	page 92	formal 'you'	حَضْرِتَك
track 026	page 96		أُسْتاذ and أُسْتاذة
track 027	page 97		حاجّ and حاجّة
track 028	page 99		مدام and آنِسة
track 029	page 100		حبيبي and حبيبْتي
track 030	page 103		كابْتِن
track 031	page 104		شيْخ
track 032	page 105		ريِّس
track 033	page 106		يافنْدِم
track 034	page 107		باشا
track 035	page 109		حَضْرة الظّابِط
track 036	page 110		دُكْتور
track 037	page 112		باشْمُهنْدِس
track 038	page 113		مِتْر
track 039	page 114		مِسْتر and مِيس
track 040	page 115		أُسْطى
track 041	page 116		يابْني and يا بِنْتي
track 042	page 118		عَمّو and طنْط
track 043	page 120		بابا and ماما
track 044	page 121		جِدّو and تيتة

حضرِتك

formal 'you'

The masculine singular حضْرِتك, feminine singular حضْرِتِك, and plural حضراتْكُم are used as more formal and respectful counterparts of the more common second-person pronouns (إِنْتَ, إِنْتِي, and إِنْتو, respectively), all of which would simply translate as you in English. Its usage depends on the situation and relationship between the speaker and addressee, as is the case in other languages that have both informal and formal second-person pronouns or speech levels (French vous; German Sie; Spanish usted; Russian вы; Turkish siz, etc.) The noun حضْرة itself is literally a title of respect: esquire, presence, etc.

حضْرِتك is used with strangers, especially if that person is older than you.

أ: ألاقي معَ حضْرِتك فكّةْ مية؟
ب: مُمْكِن خمْسينْتينْ؟
أ: تمام أيّ حاجة.

A: Can you break a hundred [-pound bill]?
B: Are two fifties okay?
A: Sure, whatever is fine.

حضرْتك is used on the telephone if you do not know who you are speaking with.

أ: ألو مُمْكِن أكلِّم مدام دُعاء؟
ب: أَيْوَه، أقولّها مين حضْرِتك؟

A: Hello, may I speak with Mrs. Doaa?
B: Yes, who shall I tell her is calling [lit. ... who you are]?

حضرْتك is used when addressing someone you know who is (a generation) older. It is even used within some families with uncles and aunts (and less commonly with one's own parents).

أ: طنْط، أنا كلِّمْت حضْرِتِك إمْبارِح بسّ حضْرِتِك مردِّتيش. أنا قُلْت أكيد مشْغولة.
ب: يا خبر! مخدْتِش بالي خالِص يا حبيبْتي. خيْر؟

A: Auntie, I called you yesterday, but you didn't answer. I figured you must be busy.
B: Oh my! I didn't notice at all, honey. What's up?

أ: كُلّ سنة و إنْتي طيِّبة يا ريم! يَلّا خُدي العيدية.
ب: و حضْرِتك طيِّب يا عمّو.

A: Happy holiday, Reem! Come on, here's your holiday gift.
B: Happy holiday, uncle!

عيدية is a gift (or money) given to children by relatives on major religious holidays.

حَضْرِتك is used when speaking with superiors in a professional context.

أ: يا بشْمُهَنْدِسة، جهّزْتي التقْرير؟
ب: أَيْوَه يافنْدِم، و بعتُّه لِحضْرِتك على المِيْل.

A: Did you finish the report yet, engineer?
B: Yes, sir, and I've emailed it to you.

حَضْرِتك is used with speaking with professionals–anyone from a plumber to a doctor.

أ: طيِّب، تِقْدر تِعدّي عليّا النّهارْده تصلّح الحنفية؟
ب: والله حضْرِتك، النّهارْده عنْدي شُغْل بسّ بُكْره الصُّبْح هكلِّمك و أجيلك على طول.

A: Well, could you come by today to repair the faucet?
B: Honestly, sir, today I'm busy, but tomorrow morning, I'll call you and come right over.

Notice, in the dialogue above, that حَضْرِتك is used vocatively (and not as a subject), so the translation is a formal form of address: sir.

أ: طيِّب، وَرّيني كِده البُقع اللي بِتِظْهر عَ الجِلْد
ب: بُصّ يا دُكْتور، دي ظهِرت مِن يومين و دي لسّه طالْعة النّهارْده الصُّبْح. حضْرِتك شايِف أيْه؟
أ: خلّينا نِعْمِل تحْليل و نْشوف. بسّ إن شاء الله بسيطة.

A: Okay, show me the blemishes on the skin.
B: See, doctor, this one appeared a couple of days ago, and this one just appeared this morning. What do you think?
A: Let's run a biopsy and see, but hopefully, it's nothing.

The plural form حَضراتْكُم is mainly used in particularly formal contexts, especially when speaking in public.

(in a speech)

و زيّ ما حضراتْكُم طبْعاً عارفين إنّ السّنة اللي فاتِت العالم كُلّه مرّ بأزْمة اقْتِصادية كْبيرة...

And as you all know, of course, last year the entire world experienced an economic crisis...

(a waiter addressing customers in a fancy restaurant)

أ: أهْلاً بيكم يافنْدِم. حضراتْكُم أوّل مرّة تْشرّفونا بِالزِّيارة؟

ب: لا دي تاني مرّة نيجي المطْعم هِنا.

A: Welcome! Is this the first time you honor us with your visit?
B: No, it's the second time we've come to the restaurant here.

There is an even more respectful word: سِيادْتِك/سِيادْتَك, which is used in especially formal situations and with those in positions of authority (politicians, judges, military generals, etc.) And diplomats are addressed as سعادْتِك/سعادْتَك.

أُسْتاذ and أُسْتاذة

We'll be taking a look at several forms of address in this section, but when in doubt, the default form of address—the most neutral, polite, and safest way to address a stranger—is أُسْتاذ (to a man) and أُسْتاذة (to a woman).

أ: خُدي بالِك يا أُسْتاذة! شنْطِتِك وِقْعِت.
ب: تمام شُكْراً!

A: Watch out, miss/ma'am! You dropped your purse.
B: Ah! Thanks!

أ: أُسْتاذ، إنْتَ كِده قافِل على الجراج.
ب: دِقيقة و طالع!

A: Sir, you're blocking the garage [entrance].
B: Just a minute, and I'll be leaving!

Notice that the vocative particle يا usually precedes forms of address (including names), but it can optionally be omitted, as seen in the example above.

حاجّ and حاجّة

حاجّ and حاجّة are honorific titles to show respect to an elderly person. The word literally means pilgrim–originally a title for someone who has completed the Islamic pilgrimage to Mecca– but its current use has nothing to do with whether that person has actually completed their pilgrimage. You can use it with anyone who has gray hair and is at least a generation older than you.

أ: اِتْفضّلي يا حاجّة باقي الفِلوس.

ب: تِسْلم يابْني.

A: Here's your change, hajja.
B: Bless you, my son.

أ: حاجّ! يا حاجّ! إنْتَ كْويِّس؟

ب: آه يابْني معلِشْ، دخْت شْويَّة.

A: Hajj! Hey, hajj! Are you okay?
B: Yes, my son. I just felt a bit dizzy.

You may hear Egyptians in rural communities (and taxi drivers!) sometimes address elderly strangers as أبويا **my father and** أمّي **my mother.**

أ: اُوْمُري يا أُمّي، عايْزة أيْه؟

ب: عايْزة تلاتة كيلو بطاطِس يابْني.

A: Yes, ma'am, what would you like?
B: I need three kilos of potatoes, my son.

أ: اِتْفضّل يا أبويا، الكُرْسي ده لِحدّ ما العربية توصل.

ب: شُكْراً يابْني.

A: Take this chair, sir, until the bus comes.
B: Thank you, my son.

آنِسة and مدام

مدام ma'am **is a form of address for a woman who you know is married or is old enough that you expect that she would be.** آنِسة miss **is for a young, unmarried woman. Remember, you can always use** أُسْتاذة **instead to avoid the risk of addressing a woman the wrong way.**

(in a fabric store)

أ: ألاقي عنْدك مِن القُماشة دي نفْس اللّوْن؟

ب: لا واللهِ يا مدام، بسّ شوفي المحلّ اللي جمْبي.

A: Do you have this same fabric in the same color?
B: No, ma'am. But you can check the store next door.

أ: أطْلع على شارِع طلعْت حرْب مْنيْن؟

ب: بُصّي يا آنِسة، هتمْشي طَوالي، في أوّل يِمين.

A: How can I get to Talaat Harb Street?
B: Well, miss, you'll go straight, then take the second right.

حبيبي and حبيبْتي

You can address a child (stranger or known) with حبيبي (for boys) and حبيبْتي (for girls) dear, darling, sweetie, honey.

(seeing an unattended child on the street)

أ: حبيبي، إنْتَ فيه حدّ معاك؟

ب: آه، ماما جُوّه المحلّ.

A: Honey, is there someone [older] with you?
B: Yes, my mom is inside the store.

(to a girl who's tripped and fallen on the street)

أ: خلّي بالِك يا حبيبْتي و إنْتي ماشْية!

ب: حاضِر.

A: Sweetie, watch out while you're walking!
B: Okay.

Although it can be freely used with small children, حبيبي and حبيبْتي should only be used with adult strangers of the same sex. That is, it would be inappropriate and ill-received for a man to address a female adult stranger as حبيبْتي.

(a woman to a veiled woman on the street)

أ: حبيبْتي، خُدي بالِك، شعْرِك باينِ.
ب: أيْه ده بِجدّ! شُكْرًا!

A: Dear, watch out. Your hair is showing.
B: Oh... yes! Thank you [for telling me]!

(a female shop assistant to a female customer)

أ: خلاص أنا هاخُد الجزْمة دي.
ب: مبْروك عليْكي. كده الحِساب ٣٥٠.
أ: تمام اِتْفضّلي حبيبْتي.

A: All right, I'll take this pair of shoes.
B: Congratulations [on the purchase]! So, the price is 350.
A: Okay, here you are, dear.

(a male passenger in a taxi)

أ: هنْزِل هِنا على جمْب.
ب: ألْف حمْدِللّه ع السّلامة يا حبيبي.
أ: حبيبي! نهارك زيّ الفُلّ.

A: I'll get out here.
B: Thank God you arrived safely at your destination, dear.
A: [Bless you!] My dear! Have a lovely morning.

However, حبيبي and حبيبْتي are used freely with the opposite sex within families, among friends, and between spouses.

أ: ما أنا قُلْتِلك يا حبيبْتي إنّ البرينْتر مِش شغّالة.
ب: طب أطْبع الحاجات دي مِنيْن دِلْوَقْتي؟
أ: شوفي كِده السّكْرتيْرة.

A: I told you, dear, the printer isn't working.
B: Where shall I print them now?
A: Check with the secretary.

أ: تِشْرب أيْه يا عمّو؟

ب: أيّ حاجة يا حبيبْتي... متِتْعِبيش نفْسِك.

A: What would you like to drink, uncle?
B: Anything, dear. Don't trouble yourself.

أ: صِحيتي يا حبيبْتي؟

ب: آه يا حبيبي، صباح الخيْر. تِفْطر؟

A: Are you awake, honey?
B: Yes, darling, I'm awake. Breakfast?

كابْتِن

كابْتِن captain is the title for trainers in clubs (soccer, judo, etc.), but it is also a friendly way to address a young man who is a stranger. It is mostly used by men.

كابْتِن، خُد بالك! فيه فْلوس وِقْعِت مِنّك!

Hey man, watch out! You dropped some money.

شيْخ

شيْخ is the title for an imam (worship leader of a mosque) and the polite form of address for religious teachers (of Quran, for example), but it is also sometimes used to address long-bearded men, whose appearance resembles that of imams.

أ: يا شيْخ... اِسْتنّى الباقي!
ب: لا خلاص، خلّيهولك.

A: Sheikh, wait for your change.
B: No, it's okay. You can keep it.

يا شيْخ can also be used sarcastically among friends when casting blame, as in حرام عليْك يا شيْخ (to a man) or يا شيْخة حرام عليكي (to a woman) 'Shame on you!'

ريِّس

ريِّس **[lit. boss, president] is usually used to address a man of higher status (stranger or acquaintance).**

أ: يا ريِّس، الباب اللي وَرا مفْتوح.
ب: تِسْلم، شُكْراً!

A: Hey, boss! The back door [of your car] is open/ajar.
B: Bless you! Thanks!

يافنْدِم

يافنْدِم is interchangeable with (يا) باشا and is commonly used by both men and women. Incidentally, it is also a word borrowed from Turkish. يافنْدِم sounds a more formal and serious than باشا. Notice that it always begins with the vocative particle يا when used as a form of address.

أ: أنا قُلْتِلت مفيش أجازات يَعْني مفيش أجازات!
ب: يافنْدِم بسّ أنا حجزْت خلاص، مَينْفعْش ألْغي حتّى.

A: I've already said it... No time off means no time off!
B: But sir, I've already made the reservation, and I cannot even cancel.

Without the vocative particle يا, أفنْدِم is an interjection used with strangers: 'Sorry?!', 'Excuse me?', 'I beg your pardon!'

أ: معلِشّ مُمْكِن حضْرِتك تِدْفعْلي علشان مِش معايا فْلوس.
ب: أفنْدِم؟ طب و حضْرِتك جيْت ليْه طالما معاكْش فْلوس؟!

A: Excuse me, could you please pay for me, as I don't have money?
B: I beg your pardon! Why did you come if you don't have any money?!

باشا

باشا (originally an honorific Ottoman title) has not been used as a formal title since Egypt became a republic. Nowadays, its use shows respect–while maintaining a friendly tone–to a man of higher status–by a service worker to a customer, etc. It is much more commonly used by men.

(a parking attendant to a man who has just gotten out of his car)

أ: هتطوّل يا باشا؟

ب: لا هركِن خمْسة بسّ و راجِع.

A: Are you staying long, sir?
B: No, I'll just be parked [here] for five minutes and then come back.

Notice that the word دقايِق minutes is unexpressed. (See p. 130).

(between a customer and the waiter)

أ: الحِساب كام؟

ب: خلّي علينا يا باشا!

أ: حبيبي تِسْلم. قولّي بسّ.

A: What do I owe you?
B: It's on us, sir!
A: Bless you, dear. Just tell me [how much].

خلّي علينا [lit. *leave it to us*] is not to be taken literally. It is merely a figure of speech embedded in the language and reflects the importance of hospitality in Egyptian culture. Think of it simply as a humble thank-you. You are still expected to pay!

(speaking with the doorman of a building)

أ: بقولّك أيْه، طلّع الكيّس ده لِأُسْتاذ مُراد اللي في العاشِر.

ب: حاضِر يا باشا.

A: Hey, take this [plastic] bag up to Mr. Murad on the tenth floor.
B: Certainly, sir.

باشا can also be used to address a police officer with respect.

أ: هتِعْمِلوا صُلْح وَلّا نِفْتح محْضر؟

ب: لا خلاص يا باشا. أنا كِده أخدْت حقّي.

A: Will you settle the matter among yourselves, or shall we file a report?
B: No, it's okay, officer. I've taken my due. [We're good now.]

حَضْرِةْ الظَّابِط

حَضْرِةْ الظَّابِط is (along with باشا, as mentioned in the previous segment) the proper way to address a police officer.

أ: يا حَضْرِةْ الظَّابِط، الكلام اللي بِيْقولُه ده مِش حقيقي.
ب: اِسْتَنّى لَمّا آخُد أقْوالك.

A: Officer, what he's saying is not true!
B: Hold on until I take your statement.

دُكْتُور

دُكْتُور and دُكْتُورة are used with medical doctors as well as professors and other Ph.D. holders. It can also be used with pharmacists. Even though pharmacists don't have doctoral degrees, per se, this form of address shows respect for them as medical professionals who do have licenses in their field.

(to a physician)

أ: بعْد التّحاليل دي هنِحْتاج نِعْمِل مِنْظار في أقْرب وَقْت.

ب: للِدّرجة دي يا دُكْتُور؟ طب إمْتى مُمْكِن أعْمِلْها؟

A: After these tests, we'll need to do an endoscopy as soon as possible.
B: Is it that serious, doctor? Then, when can I have it done?

(to a pharmacist)

أ: دُكْتُورة، ألاقي عنْدِك أيّ دَوا الصُّداع؟

ب: مُمْكِن تاخُد مُسكِّن.

A: Pharmacist, do you have anything for a headache?
B: You could take a painkiller.

(to a professor)

أ: دُكْتورْ، الاِمْتِحان الشَّفَوي عليْه كام درجة؟

ب: ٢٥ درجة. و التّحْريري ٥٠ و الأبْحاث ٢٥.

A: Professor, what percentage of the grade is the oral exam?
B: 25. And the written [exam] is 50, and the research paper is 25.

باشْمُهَنْدِس

باشْمُهَنْدِس and باشْمُهَنْدِسة [lit. head engineer] are used with engineers, architects, and interior designers.

(speaking with a decorator)

أ: باقي قدّ أيْه عَ التّسْليم يا بشْمُهَنْدِس؟
ب: ها إنْتَ واللهِ باقي التّشْطيبات الأخيرة.

A: How much time is left for delivery, engineer?
B: We're almost there, really. Just some final touches are left.

مِتْر

مِتْر [from the French 'maître'] is used with lawyers (mostly with male lawyers).

أ: طب فيه أمل في البراءة، مِتْر؟
ب: إن شاء الله الجلْسة الجايّة الرُّؤْيَة هتْبان.

A: Is there any hope in proving innocence, lawyer?
B: Hopefully, during the next hearing, things will become clear.

It is also used to address waiters in very fancy restaurants.

أ: مِتْر! الحِساب مِن فضْلك.
ب: أيّ أَوامِر تانْيَة حضْرِتك؟
أ: لأ كلُّه تمام.

A: Waiter! Check, please!
B: Is there anything else, sir?
A: No, everything's fine.

مِسْتر and ميس

ميس and مِسْتر (from the English 'mister' and 'miss') are forms of address used with teachers in institutes, universities, as well as primary and secondary schools–although, in public (government) primary and secondary schools, it is more common to address teachers with أُسْتاذ and أُسْتاذة. These forms of address can be used alone or followed by the teacher's first name.

أ: صباح الخيْر، مِسْتر حُسام.
ب: صباح النّور. ياسْمين، عملْتي الواجِب؟

A: Good morning, Mr. Hossam!
B: Good morning! Yasmine, have you done your homework?

أ: ميس! مُمْكِن أروح الحمّام؟
ب: اِتْفضّل و متِتْأخّرْش.

A: Teacher, can I go to the bathroom?
B: Go ahead, but don't take too long.

In the past (and perhaps still in some rural areas), female teachers were addressed as أَبْلة (a Turkish word meaning *older sister*).

أُسْطى

أُسْطى is the proper form of address for a man who is a skilled worker–such as a mechanic, carpenter, or taxi driver–but does not have an advanced degree (such as a doctor or lawyer). Notice the merged pronunciation when preceded by the vocative particle: ياسْطى.

(in a taxi)

أ: على جمْب ياسْطى.
ب: اتْفضّلي يا حاجّة.

A: Please stop here, driver.
B: Here you are, ma'am.

(to a plumber)

أ: طيِّب تقْدر تعدّي عليّا النّهارْده تصلّح الحنفية ياسْطى؟
ب: والله حضرْتِك النّهارْده عنْدي شغْل بسّ بُكْره الصُّبْح هكلِّمِك و أجيلِك على طول.

A: Well, could you come by today to fix the faucet?
B: Ma'am, I'm really quite busy today, but tomorrow morning I'll call you and come over right away.

يا بِنْتي and يابْني

You can address someone who is a generation younger than you in a familiar style, as يابْني my son or يا بِنْتي my daughter.

أ: اِتْفضّلي يا بِنْتي، اقْعُدي. أنا نازِل المحطّة الجايّة.
ب: شُكراً يا حاجّ، تِسْلم.

A: Here you are, young lady. Have a seat. I'm getting off at the next station.
B: Thank you, hajj. Bless you.

يابْني and يا بِنْتي are also used among friends and siblings as a very casual form of address.

أ: يابْني، أنا مِش قُلْتِلك هنْروح سَوا؟
ب: أيْه ده بِجدّ؟ مخدْتِش بالي خالِص.

A: Dude! Didn't I tell you we'd go together?
B: What? Seriously? I was not aware.

There are a number of other ways to address a friend casually (or sarcastically), including يا سيدي, يا عمّ, **and** يا خويا **for men, and** يا هانِم, ياخْتي, يا سِتّي **and for women.**

أ: بقولَّك أيْه، مِش هنِتْحايِل عليْك كتِير. يَلّا علشان نُخْرُج!

ب: ماشي يا خويا!

A: Hey! We're not going to keep insisting, but come on! Let's go out!
B: Okay, bro!

طنْط and عمّو

عمّو uncle and طنْط auntie are polite but informal forms of address for adults who are a generation older than you—neighbors, family friends, your friends' parents, or even strangers (especially by children).

سامِحْني يا عمّو، مِش هقْدر آجي... تعْبان أوي.

Forgive me, uncle. I won't be able to make it. I'm not feeling well.

أ: إزّيِّك يا طنْط؟ و إزّي صِحِّتِك؟
ب: الحمْدُ لِلّه حبيبتي. طمّنيني عليْكُم إنْتو.

A: How are you, auntie? How's your health?
B: Thank God, my dear. And tell me how you all are doing.

In rural communities, you may hear خالْتي instead of طنْط.

Now, let's take a look at how to address our actual aunts and uncles in the family. In Arabic, a distinction is made between paternal and maternal aunts and uncles. You call your father's brother عمّو, your father's sister عمّتو, your mother's brother خالو, and your mother's sister خالْتو. In English, we would also consider their spouses our uncles and aunts, but as there are no special terms in Arabic for these people, we would address them as we do non-relatives who are a generation older—as عمّو and طنْط.

أ: يا عمِّتو، بقولِّك والله شبْعانة!
ب: مَينْفعْش، لازِم تاكْلي معانا.

A: Aunt, I'm telling you, I'm really full.
B: No way! You must eat with us.

ليْه بسّ يا خالو مجيتْش إمْبارِح؟

Why didn't you come over yesterday, uncle?

There are variations and preferences in each family when it comes to how to call aunts and uncles. In some middle- or upper-class families, uncle is أونْكل, for example.

إزَّيِّك يا أونْكل؟ وَحشْتِني!

How are you doing, uncle? I missed you!

In rural communities, variations with ـي endings are more common (عمِّي، خالْتي, etc.), and their usage may be extended to a father-in-law, sister-in-law, and so on.

(speaking to a neighbor lady)

أ: كُلّ سنة و إنْتي طيِّبة يا خالْتي! رمضان بُكْره.
ب: و إنْتي طيِّبة يا بنْتي! الجُمْعة الجايّة الفِطار عنْدِنا.

A: Happy holidays, auntie! Ramadan is tomorrow.
B: To you too, my daughter. Next Friday, iftar [breaking of the fast] is at our place.

ماما and بابا

بابا dad and ماما mom are the most common ways Egyptians address their parents, especially in urban communities.

بابا، مُمْكِن تِوَصَّلْني بُكْره بِاللّيْل؟

Dad, can you drive me tomorrow evening?

لا يا ماما، سارة لِسّه مجتْش مِن برّه.

No, Mom, Sara isn't home yet.

Of course, there are variations depending on the family and social class. Among the upper-class, borrowings from English are common: مامي mommy, بابي pappy, دادي daddy. Among the working class and in rural communities, you may hear يامّة mom and يابا dad.

تيْتة and جدّو

جِدّو grandpa and تيْتة (or نيْنة) grandma are commonly used by all Egyptians. You may hear سِتّو or سِتّي for grandma, but it's much less common.

تيْتة، وَحشْتيني أوي!
I miss you so much, Grandma!

بقولّك يا جِدّو، فاضي بُكْره أعدّي عليْك؟
Hey, Grandpa, are you free tomorrow if I come by?

Section 4
Numbers in Idioms

There are numerous idioms in Egyptian Arabic that contain numbers. Some are straightforward and logical. Others seem as if there must be a story behind them, but Egyptians usually have little idea why this or that number is used in a particular idiom; they just use them without questioning them too much. In English, why do we say 'on cloud nine,' 'in seventh heaven,' 'at sixes and sevens'? The point is, don't worry too much about the history and logic behind such idioms. Just learn them and their meanings. A third kind of idiom with numbers is the hyperbole, where any large number would do, but Egyptians have some favorites, as you'll see in this section.

track 045	page 124	Slow down!	واحْدة واحْدة
track 046	page 125	one, two, three…	الله واحِد…
track 047	page 126	What's the third of three?	تِلْت التّلاتة كامْ؟
track 048	page 127	a third tripled-up	تالِت و مْتلِّت
track 049	page 128	the third is final	التّالْتة تابْتة
track 050	page 130	five minutes	خمْسة
track 051	page 131	Knock on wood!	خمْسة و خميسة

track 052	page 132	to be beside oneself	ضرب أخْماس في أسْداس
track 053	page 133	'donuts'	خمْسات
track 054	page 134	to search and search	لفّ سبع لفّات
track 055	page 135	with seven lives	بِسبع تَرْواح
track 056	page 136	in a deep sleep	في سابِع نوْمة
track 057	page 137	we're all equal	كُلنا ولاد تِسْعة
track 058	page 138	'full moon'	قمر أربعْتاشر
track 059	page 139	It's useless!	ملهاش تلاتين لازْمة
track 060	page 140	centipede	أم أرْبعة و أرْبعين
track 061	page 141	Go to hell!	في سِتّين داهْية
track 062	page 143	Son of a … !	إبْن سِتّين في سبْعين
track 063	page 144	110 jasmine flowers	مية فُلّ و عشرة
track 064	page 145	300 welcomes!	يا تلْتمية مرْحبا
track 065	page 146	a zillion times	عشرومية مرّة
track 066	page 148	A thousand congratulations!	ألْف مبْروك
track 067	page 149	A thousand thanks!	ألْف شُكْر
track 068	page 150	Welcome back!	ألْف حمْدلله ع السّلامة

واحْدة واحْدة

Slow down!

واحْدة واحْدة [lit. one by one] is used to get someone to slow down when giving information (spelling, numbers, steps, directions, etc.)

أ: بُصّ سجِّل الرّقم ده عنْدك: صِفْر، خمْسِتينْ، تلات تمانْيات، مِتينْ أرْبعة و سِتّينْ...

ب: بِالرّاحة بسّ، واحْدة واحْدة... قول تاني كِده.

A: Hey, save this [serial] number: zero – five five – eight eight eight – two hundred sixty-four...

B: Hold on a moment! Slow down and tell me again.

الله واحِد، ملوش تاني، بركة التّلاتة...

one, two, three...

You may hear some very religious people start counting money by invoking God as in this expression, literally God is 'one'... He has no 'second'... blessed is 'the [number] three'...

أ: بقولّك أيْه، عِدّ دولْ كِده شوفْهُم ألْف.
ب: الله واحِد... ملوش تاني... بركة التّلاتة... أرْبعة... خمْسة...

A: Hey, count these [bills] and check if it's 1,000.
B: One, two, three, four five...

تِلْت التَّلاتة كامْ؟

What's the third of three?

This idiom implies that someone cannot utter a word—the cat's got their tongue; they're tongue-tied. The second line in the dialogue literally means that he couldn't [even] say 'What's the third of three?'–that is, he couldn't even articulate a simple thought.

أ: بسّ إنْتَ كِده زنقْتُه، أكيد معْرِفْش يِرُدّ عليْك.
ب: وَلا عِرِف يِقول تِلْت التَّلاتة كامْ.

A: But you put him in a tight spot. He definitely couldn't reply to you.
B: He couldn't say a word.

تالِت و مُتلِّت

a third tripled-up

تالِت و مُتلِّت [lit. a third and tripled] means whole and sound (leaving no bit of it).

أ: و هتْسيب حقّك كده يضيع منّك؟
ب: لا طبْعاً... هاخُد حقّي مِنهُم تالِت و مُتلِّت.

A: And will you give up what's yours?
B: Of course not! I will take every last bit of my due from them.

التّالْتة تابْتة

the third is final

This expression is very common. It expresses that the third time is final, the limit, or too much.

أ: مِش ناوي تِتِّصِل تِعْرِف اتْقبِلْت في الإنْتِرْڤْيو ولّا لأ؟
ب: لا خلاص التّالْتة تابْتة. كلِّمْتُهُم مرِّتين قبْل كِده و موَصِلْتِش لِحاجة.

A: Aren't you going to call them to see if you've been accepted for the interview?
B: No way. Three is final. I already called them twice and got nowhere.

The Modern Standard Arabic word ثابِت fixed, stable becomes سابِت in Egyptian Arabic, but in the set expression التّالْتة تابْتة, it is pronounced with ت for alliteration.

يَلا نْدوِّر على المُفْتاح مرّة تالْتة. و التّالْتة تابْتة.
Let's look for the key again. One final time!

دي تالِت مرّة نِفْشل. خلاص بقى، التّالْتة تابْتة.

This is the third time we've failed. That's it; we've tried enough.

إنْتَ كِده ضربْتِني مرِّتيْن و سِبْتك. بسّ التّالْتة تابْتة!

You've hit me three times, and I let it go. But the third time, I'm going to hit back!

خَمْسة

five minutes

In this expression, five is an arbitrary number. It really means a few minutes and shouldn't be taken too literally, of course. Notice that the word for 'minutes' is dropped, so you're just saying 'five.'

أ: معلِشّ يا أُسْتاذ مِدْحت. أسْتأذنك مِحْتاج مُراد خمْسة بسّ.

ب: تمام بسّ متأخّروش علشان بنِشْتغل في حاجات مُهِمّة.

A: Excuse me, Mr. Medhat. I just need Mourad for five minutes.
B: Sure, but don't keep him long. We're working on important stuff.

خمْسة و خميسة

Knock on wood!

While most Egyptians believe in the evil eye (since it's a Quranic concept), belief in the power of the digit '5' to protect against the evil eye is folk superstition. Those who do believe in this may use the expression خمْسة و خميسة sincerely to ward off the evil eye. However, many people use it sarcastically or playfully, much as English speakers might use 'knock on wood.' خميسة is a (usually blue) amulet of an open hand with an eye in the palm.

أ: بسّ أيْه الشّقّة الحِلْوَة دي بسّ!
ب: خمْسة و خميسة ياخْتي! ما تْصلّيْ عَ النّبي.

A: What a fancy apartment!
B: Five, girl! Pray for the Prophet!

See p. 167 to find out what the speaker above should have said to avoid her friend's reaction.

ضرْب أخْماس في أسْداس

to be beside oneself

ضرب أخْماس في أسْداس [lit: to multiply fifths by sixths] refers to being super confused with absolutely no clue what to do, be frozen from shock

(B telling that he realized he'd forgotten his passport when he got to the airport)

أ: طبّ و عملْت أيْه مِن غيْر الباسْبورْ؟

ب: قعدْت أضْرب أخْماس في أسْداس... و رْجِعْت. هعْمِل أيْه يَعْني؟

A: And what did you do without a passport?

B: I had no clue what to do, so I went back [home]. What [else] could I do?

خَمْسات

'donuts'

The number 'five' can take a plural ending to refer to circular skid marks (donuts), since the digit ٥ (5) is a circle in Arabic.

أ: مُمْكِن بَعْد ما أتْعلِّم سِواقة تِسيبْني أعْمِل شْوَيّة خَمْسات؟

ب: طبّ اتِعلِّم الأوّل بسّ و بعْدينْ نِشوف مَوْضوع الخَمْسات.

A: Will you let me do some donuts after I learn how to drive?
B: Just learn first, and then we can see about the donuts thing.

لفّ سبع لفّات

to search and search

The idiom لفّ سبع لفّات and its interchangeable synonym داخ سبع دَوْخات invoke a picture of someone getting dizzy from turning and turning, having to go around from place to place, being given the run-around, or looking everywhere searching for something.

أ: وِصِلْتي لْحاجة في شْهادة الضّمان؟
ب: اِسْكْتي... أنا لفّيْت سبع لفّات و مَوْصِلْتِش لِأيّ حاجة.

A: Did you reach any consensus about the warranty?
B: Don't ask. I went around and around but to no avail.

بِسبع ترْواح

with seven lives

If we say someone is بِسبع ترْواح [lit. with seven souls], we mean that they come out unscathed from treacherous situations. In English, we'd say they have nine lives (like a cat).

أ: حمْدِلله على سلامْتك يا وَحْش! إنْتَ غاوي تِخُضْنا عليْك وَلّا أيْه؟

ب: لا أنا زيّ القُطط بِسبع ترْواح. متقْلقْش!

A: Thank God you're safe [after a health scare], tough guy. Do you want to scare us?

B: No, I'm just like cats—with seven souls. Don't worry!

يا وَحْش [lit. monster] has a positive connotation here and implies that you are strong and resilient enough to overcome adversity. It is usually used with men and is interchangeable with يا بطل.

The plural of روح *soul* is أرْواح, but in some plural nouns, an initial vowel changes to تـ after a number.

في سابِع نوْمة

in a deep sleep

The idiom في سابِع نوْمة literally means in the seventh sleep, implying a very deep level of sleep.

أ: بابا صاحي؟

ب: لا ده تِلاقيه في سابِع نوْمة دِلْوَقْتي.

A: Is dad awake?
B: No, he's deep in sleep now.

كُلِّنا وِلاد تِسْعة

we're all equal

كُلِّنا وِلاد تِسْعة [lit. we are all children of nine] is a reminder that we are all human, born after <u>nine</u> months in the womb—"children of nine."

أ: إنْتَ مَعْووج كِده ليْه؟ ما كُلِّنا وِلاد تِسْعة.
ب: وَلا مَعْووج وَلا حاجة!

A: Why are you so arrogant? We're all 'children of nine.'
B: I'm not arrogant whatsoever!

قمر أرْبعْتاشر

'full moon'

قمر moon is an epithet for a beautiful woman. In the Islamic (Hijri) lunar calendar, months begin with a new moon, meaning the full moon is halfway–on the 14th of the month, so قمر أرْبعْتاشر moon of the 14th emphasizes that she is incredibly beautiful.

أ: و أيْه رأيِك فيها يا ماما؟
ب: قمر أرْبعْتاشر. ربِّنا يِسْعِدْكُم يا حبيبي.

A: And what do you think about her, Mom?
B: She's absolutely gorgeous. May God grant you happiness, dear.

ملْهاش تلاتين لازْمة

It's useless!

ملْهاش تلاتين لازْمة [lit. it doesn't have thirty uses] is recent slang popular among young Egyptians.

أ: أنا بفكّر أعْمِل دِبْلوْمة تربَوي.
ب: وَلا ليها أيّ تلاتين لازْمة في مجالْنا.

A: I'm thinking of pursuing a pedagogy degree.
B: That's of no use at all in our field.

أُمّ أَرْبعة و أَرْبعين

centipede

أُمّ أَرْبعة و أَرْبعين [lit. having forty-four (legs)] is the Arabic word for centipede. But if you call a woman a 'centipede' in Egyptian Arabic, you mean that she is sneaky and not to be trusted–like calling someone 'a snake' in English.

أ: إنْتي بْتِرْتاحي لِطنْط فَوْقية دي؟
ب: دي سِتّ أعوذ بِالله... أُمّ أَرْبعة و أَرْبعين.

A: Do you feel comfortable with this Auntie Faw'eyya?
B: What a vicious woman she is! Such a sneaky snake!

أعوذ بِالله [lit. *I seek refuge in God*] is a shortened form of أعوذ بِالله مِن الشّيْطان الرّجيم [lit. *I seek protection in God from Satan the reviled*], which is often uttered before reading the Quran, when hit with evil thoughts, when waking up from a nightmare, and so on. In Egyptian Arabic, it is also an epithet (as in the dialogue above) that indicates you consider the person or thing mentioned to be 'evil.'

في سِتّين داهْيَة

Go to hell!

The number 'sixty' is always used in negative, angry connotations.

أ: كمال بِيْقول إنُّه مِش قادِر يِكمِّل معانا علشان ضغْط الشُّغْل.

ب: في سِتّين داهْيَة.

A: Kamal says he's not going to be able to stay on with us [in the company] because of the pressure of the job.
B: Let him go to hell then!

أ: يَعْني ده آخِر كلام عنْدك؟ طب أنا ماشي و وَرّوني هتْكمِّلوا مِن غيْري إزّاي!

ب: في سِتّين داهْيَة يا حبيبي! الباب يِفوِّت جمل!

A: So, that's your final say? Okay, I'm out of here. Show me just how you're going to [be able to] finish this without me!
B: Go to hell, my dear! The door is wide open [for you to leave]!

The expression used here الباب يِفوّت جمل literally means 'the door (is big enough to) let a camel pass through it.' That is, 'Nothing's stopping you! Leave!'

إبْن سِتّين في سبْعين

Son of a ... !

As we saw with the previous expression, the number 'sixty' has a negative connotation in idioms. إبْن سِتّين في سبْعين [lit. son of sixty times seventy] **is a term of contempt: son of a &#%! Although not polite, it is less vulgar than** ابْن كلْب [lit. son of a dog] **or** ابْن سِتّين كلْب [lit. son of sixty dogs].

أ: شُفْت عِماد عمل أيْه بعْد ما طلّق مِراته؟
ب: عِرِفْت. ده إبْن سِتّين في سبْعين عايِز الحرْق!

A: Did you hear what Emad did after he divorced his wife?
B: I heard. He's a son of a &#%! and deserves to be set on fire!

The terms above are some of the least vulgar terms of contempt. There are expressions that can get much more vulgar and offensive. We won't list them here! But just know that anything following يعْلِن الـ 'damn...', يابْن الـ 'son of a...', بِنْت الـ 'daughter of a...', or يا ولاد الـ 'children of a...' is a vulgar term of contempt.

ميةْ فُلّ و عشرة

110 jasmine flowers

فُلّ jasmine (flower) **is used in idioms to mean** perfect, wonderful.
A playful hyperbole is 110 jasmine flowers: ميةْ فُلّ و عشرة

أ: تِحِبّوا أنزِلُكُم دوْر شاي كمان معَ الحِلوْ؟
ب: لا كِده ميةْ فُلّ و عشرة.

A: Would you like me to serve you another round of tea with the dessert?
B: No, this is perfect (as is).

Other expressions with فُلّ:

صباح الفُلّ is a friendly response to صباح الخيْر.
زيّ الفُلّ means *lovely, perfect, wonderful*.

يا تُلْتُمية مرْحبا

300 welcomes!

أ: يا أهْلاً يا أهْلاً! يا تُلْتُمية مرْحبا.
ب: معلِشّ اتْأخّرْنا عليْكم على بال ما لقيْنا ركْنة.

A: Welcome, welcome! Three hundred welcomes!
B: Sorry we're late. It took us some time to find a parking spot.

You can also tone down the hyperbole a bit by saying
يا مية مرْحبا [lit. one hundred welcomes].

عَشْرُومِيَة مَرَّة

a zillion times

Any large number can be used arbitrarily as hyperbole. 'Fifty' and 'one hundred' are favorites: خَمْسِين مَرَّة [lit. fifty times], مِيَة مَرَّة a hundred times.

أ: أحُطّ كام معْلقة دِقيق؟
ب: ما قُلْتِلك خمْسين مرّة قبْل كِده. بِنحُطّ معْلقتيْن.

A: How many spoons of flour should I add?
B: I've told you a dozen/hundred times. We put two spoons.

أ: ما خلاص يا عمّ، سِمِعْنا الأغْنية دي ميةْ مرّة!
ب: مِعلِّقة معايا أوي!

A: Come on, dude! We've listened to this song a hundred times already!
B: It's really stuck in my head!

Not enough hyperbole for you? Try the made-up number عشْرومية [lit. ten hundred].

أ: أنا مِش طايِق اللي إسْمُه سامِح ده.
ب: يا عمّ حرامّ عليْك. الرّاجِل اعْتذرْلك عشْروميةْ مرّة. خلاص بقى.

A: I can't stand that guy named Sameh.
B: Come on, man! Shame on you. The guy has apologized to you a zillion times. Get over it.

ألف مبْروك

A thousand congratulations!

ألف one thousand **is also used as hyperbole but always with positive, happy connotations.**

أ: خُطوبْتي الأسْبوع الجّاي إن شاء اللّه و إنْتَ أكيد معْزومٍ.

ب: ألْف ألْف مبْروك يا حبيبي! ربِّنا يِتِمِّمْلك على خيْرٍ.

A: My engagement party is next week, God willing, and of course, you're invited.

B: A thousand congratulations, dear! May God fulfill it beautifully.

أَلْف شُكْر

A thousand thanks!

أ: أنا خلاص ظبّطْتِلك معاد الطيّارة. كِده تِقْدر تِطْلع عَ المطار على طول بُكْرا.

ب: ألْف شُكْرا!

A: I've already arranged the flight schedule for you. Now you can go directly to the airport tomorrow.
B: A thousand thanks!

ألْف حمْدِلله عَ السّلامة

Welcome back!

أ: أيْه ده؟ رِجِعْت مصْر إمْتى؟
ب: لِسّه مِن أُسْبوعينْ.
أ: ألْف حمْدِلله عَ السّلامة، حبيبي!

A: What's this? When did you get back to Egypt?
B: Just two weeks ago.
A: A thousand praises are due to God for your safe return, dear!

Section 5

God

الله Allah is the Arabic name for God. It's important to note that it's used to refer to God not only by Muslims but also by Christians and Jews. The word originally comes from إله god and, with the addition of the definite article ال, has taken on the unique form الله: the [one and only] God

Unlike most other Arabs, however, Egyptians almost always refer to God as ربّنا our Lord and rarely say الله except in set expressions and proverbs or when swearing. Note that, while some Christians in the West might take issue with "using the Lord's name in vain"–even in expressions such as "Oh my God!"–it is not offensive to do so for Arabs. In fact, the word الله is, on its own, a common interjection in Egyptian Arabic and has acquired a variety of meanings to express different feelings as in the first expression presented in this section.

track 069	page 153	God!	الله!
track 070	page 157	By God!	واللهِ
track 071	page 162	God Willing!	إن شاء الله
track 072	page 167	... and the Evil Eye	ما شاء الله
track 073	page 170	Praise be to God!	الحمْدُ لله
track 074	page 176	Reliance on God	التوكّل على الله
track 075	page 179	May God make it easy!	ربّنا يْسهّل
track 076	page 181	Damn you!	ربّنا ياخْدك
track 077	page 182	May God be generous with you!	ربّنا يِكرِمك

الله!

God!

الله, with an exaggeratedly long vowel, can express admiration or amazement upon seeing something beautiful (scenery, etc.).

أ: الله! بجدّ المنْظر مِن هنا تُحْفة!
ب: قُلْتِلِك الشّقّة دي مطلّاتْها أحْلى بِكْتير.

A: Oh my God! The view is magnificent from here!
B: I told you this apartment's views are way better.

أ: الله! حِلْو أوي الفُسْتان ده! جِبْتيه مْنين؟
ب: جِبْته مِن سيتي سْتارْز الإسْبوع اللي فات.

A: Wow! That dress is so beautiful! Where did you get it?
B: I got it at City Stars last week.

City Stars is a popular shopping mall in Heliopolis, Cairo Governorate.

Pronounced quickly, الله can express surprise at something unexpected and is interchangeable with يوهْ! and أيّه دهْ؟.

أ: اللهّ! إنْتَ مِش قُلْت إنَّك هتِتْأخّر النّهارْده في الشُّغْل؟

ب: ما أنا تعِبْت و أخدْت إذْن بدْري.

A: What?! Didn't you say you would be working late today?
B: Yes, but I didn't feel well and got off early.

أ: أنا زهِقْت بْجدّ مِن السِّواقة كُلّ يوْم!

ب: اللّه! مِش كُنْتي هتْموتي و تْطلّعي رُخْصة؟!

A: I'm so fed up with driving every day!
B: Huh?! Weren't you dying to get your driver's license?

When uttered once with an extended, sarcastic tone or twice slowly, الله implies blame, doubt, or 'I caught you!' It is interchangeable with يا سلام.

أ: اللّه اللّه! هُوَّ ده اللي هنْذاكِر يا ماما لِحدّ ما تِرْجعي.

ب: لا واللهِ كُنّا بِنْذاكِر بسّ أخدْنا بْريك مِن شُوَيّة و قُلْنا نِلْعب بْلاي سْتيْشن.

A: Well, well! And you told me, "We'll study, Mom, until you get back!"
B: No, really! We were studying, but we're just taking a break and thought we'd play some Playstation.

أ: الله! مِن إمْتى إن شاء الله بِتِدّي رقمك لِزمايْلك؟
ب: ده مِش رقمي الشّخْصي يابْني. ده الخطّ التّاني بْتاع الشُّغْل.

A: What's this now? Since when do you give out your [personal] phone number to your coworkers?
B: This isn't my personal number, buddy. It's a second line [I got] for work.

When repeated several times quickly, الله emphasizes the emotion expressed by the speaker's tone, whether it be disbelief, annoyance, or amazement. It is sometimes uttered so quickly that it runs together like one long word: "Allallallallah!"

(Listen to several ways this phrase may be pronounced.)
الله الله الله!

أ: لا! انْسى إنّي أسافِر معاكُم تاني!
ب: الله الله الله! أيْه اللي حصل بسّ؟! إحْنا زعّلْناكي في أيّ سفرية قبْل كِده؟

A: No way! Forget about me ever traveling with you guys again!
B: Whoa! What happened?! Have we ever given you a hard time on a trip before?

أ: خلاص أنا قرّبْت أدُقّ المِسْمار أهُه و أعلّق السّاعة... الله الله الله!
ب: خيْر؟ أيْه اللي حصل؟
أ: الشّاكوش اتْقطم!

A: This is it! I'm almost done hammering this nail and hanging the clock... Ah, shoot!
B: What is it? What happened?
A: The hammer broke!

أ: الله الله الله! يَعْني إنْتي كُوَيِّسة أهُه و مِش عيّانة!
ب: بِصراحة آه، أنا كُوَيِّسة بسّ مليش مزاج أخْرُج معاكُم.
أ: طبّ بعْد كِده بسّ مفيش داعي لِللّفّ و الدَّوَران.

A: Well, well, well! So, you're all good and not sick!
B: To tell you the truth, I'm fine. I just didn't feel like going out with you.
A: All right, but in the future, you don't need to make stuff up.

اللّفّ و الدَّوَران [lit. *turning and revolving*] means dancing around a subject without confronting it directly.

واللهِ

By God!

By adding و to الله, we have an oath that essentially means (I swear) by God. Notice that واللهِ is pronounced with a kasra (ِ) at the end.

The basic and most common usage of واللهِ is to emphasize the truthfulness of a statement and is not meant to be taken literally as an oath.

أ: بِجدّ هتِقْدري بُكْره تيجي معايا للدُّكْتور؟
ب: واللهِ فاضْيَة يا حبيبْتي. لَوْ مشْغولة كُنْت هقولِّك.

A: Can you really come with me to the doctor tomorrow?
B: I swear, I'm free, honey. If I were busy, I would have told you.

أ: بِجدّ واللهِ ده كِتير! مِش معْقول كُلّ الشُّغْل ده عليَّا لوَحْدي.

ب: طبّ ما تُرْفُضْ يابْني تاخُد شُغْل جْديد طالما مَضْغوط.

أ: مِش بِمزاجي والله... بسّ هيَّ بْتِمْشي كِده اللي بيِفْهم أكْتر بيْشيل أكْتر!

A: Seriously, I swear to God, this is too much! There's no way all this work is all my responsibility.
B: Why don't you reject new tasks as long as you're overloaded?
A: It's not actually up to me. But that's how it works. Whoever is more skillful gets more tasks!

أ: يا أخي إنْتَ عُمْرك ما تْقول كِلْمة حِلْوَة؟!

ب: بُصّ، الكَلام الحِلْو اللي بجدّ معنْديش مُشْكِلة فيه، إنّما المُجامَلات الكدّابة مليش فيها والله.

A: Hey, don't you ever say anything nice?
B: Well, look, I really don't have a problem with saying nice things that are sincere, but I'm not into fake compliments, really.

It can soften a short response and may not always need to be translated.

أ: سيجارة؟

ب: لا والله مبدخّنْش.

A: Cigarette?
B: Oh, no... I don't smoke.

أ: هتْروح الحفْلة؟
ب: والله ناوي، بسّ بحاوِل أظبّط ظُروفي.

A: Are you going to the party?
B: I intend to, but I'm trying to rearrange my schedule.

In a questioning tone, often preceded by لا, it expresses surprise or disbelief.

أ: تخيّل شُفْت مين إمْبارِح!
ب: مين؟
أ: مُحْسِن اللي كان معانا في سكْشِن رابْعة.
ب: لا والله؟! ده اخْتفى فجْأة بعْد ما اتْخرّجْنا سنين!

A: Guess who I saw yesterday!
B: Who?
A: Mohsen, who was with us during senior year.
B: No way! He suddenly disappeared after we graduated–for years!

أ: تِعْرفي، نِفْسي أطْلع مُضيفة.
ب: لا والله؟ طبّ خِسّي الأوّل و بعْدْين اِبْقي اِتْكلّمي!

A: You know, I hope to become a flight attendant.
B: Oh really? Well, lose some weight first before you say that!

والله is used to insist that someone accept an invitation or hospitality. Here, it is taken as an actual oath, and as such, should not be used too casually, especially with people you don't know well. Breaking an oath to God is a sin in Islam (which Muslims have to expiate through charity or fasting). This puts added, unwanted pressure on people to accept the invitation.

أ: طيّب قوليلي إنتي نازْلة فيْن بالظّبْط في المهنْدِسين.
ب: لا يا بِنْتي خلاص بِجدّ، متْحيّريش نفْسِك. أنا هنْزِل هِنا و أرْكب و إنْتي روّحي.
أ: لا والله أبدًا. لازِم أوَصّلِك. الجوّ صعْب و مِش هتْلاقي حاجة تِرْكبيها.

A: Tell me where exactly I should drop you off in Mohandeseen.
B: No, it's okay, dear! Seriously, you don't need to bother yourself. I'll get out here and take [some transportation], and you can go on.
A: I insist! I have to drive you. The weather is really bad, and you won't [easily] find anything [any transportation] to take.

أ: بجدّ كانت قعْدة جميلة. يا ريْت نِعْمِلْها كلّ أُسْبوع.
ب: آه بْجدّ! لازِم نِكرّرْها... إنْتَ بْتِعْمِل أيْه؟
أ: لا خلاص عليّا المرّة دي.
ب: لا والله ما يِحْصل! المرّة دي الحِساب عليّا و اِبْقى اعْزِمْني المرّة الجايّة يا سيدي.

A: That was really fun meeting up. I wish we could do it every week.
B: Yeah, definitely! We have to do it again. Ah, what are you doing?
A: Uh, uh! It's on me this time.
B: I swear, that's not happening! This time it's on me. You can get it next time, bro.

أ: والله لانْتَ لانْتَ متْغدّي معانا النّهارْده.
ب: اُعْذُرْني بِجدّ مِش هقْدر. يادوْب ألْحق معادي.
أ: لا خلاص، أنا حِلِفْت... اِتْغدّى و بعْديْن روح معادك.

A: By God! You absolutely must have lunch with us today.
B: Forgive me, but I won't be able to. I'll barely make my appointment.
A: No way! I've sworn already [I insist]! Have lunch, then go to your appointment.

In the last example above, والله is followed by لـ, which expresses a wish or desire–here, we see لـ plus إنْتَ. We could also translate the sentence as I wish you'd have lunch with us today.

إن شاء الله

God Willing!

إن شاء الله inshallah **literally means** 'if God wills [it]'–**and is commonly translated as** God willing. **It is originally a religious expression used as an acknowledgment that only God knows what will happen in the future. But it has taken many other layers of meaning in everyday Egyptian Arabic, both sincere and ironic.**

إن شاء الله **expresses a willingness to make plans, implying some assertiveness and giving the feeling that there is indeed a plan, and, as long as it is in God's will, it will be accomplished.**

أ: هتروح النّادي إمْتى؟
ب: الخميس الجاي إن شاء اللّه.

A: When will you go to the club?
B: Next Thursday, God willing.

In this sincere and original use, إن شاء الله is interchangeable with بِإذْن المَوْلى and بِإذْن الله.

إن شاء الله **can be used in a promise/commitment, but when repeated, it implies a bit less certainty:** probably, most likely.

> أ: هتيجي معانا؟ وَلّا زيّ كُلّ مرّة؟
>
> ب: لا، إن شاء اللّه، إن شاء اللّه. المرّة دي هتظْبُط معايا.

A: Will you join us? Or as usual, not?
B: No, God willing, it will work with me this time [that is, I'll be able to make it work that I can join you].

Said in a sarcastic tone, إن شاء الله **can mean** not in a million years, yeah, right!

> أ: بابا، أنا عايِز ألْف جِنيْه عشان أشْتِري سمّاعات جِديدة.
>
> ب: إن شاء اللّه حبيبي و مالُه!

A: Dad, I need 1000 LE to buy new headphones.
B: (sarcastically) Sure! Why not!

See also p. 65 and p. 88.

إن شاء الله **can also mean** hopefully, I hope.

> أ: أخْبار الامْتِحان أيْه؟
>
> ب: الحمْدُ لِلّه، هعدّي إن شاء اللّه.

A: How was the exam?
B: Good. Hopefully, I'll pass.

إن شاء الله is used to console someone and give them hope about a tough situation.

أ: أيه يابْني مُخْتِفي فيْن؟
ب: أنا في دوّامة بقالي أُسْبوع. أبويا تِعِب جامِد و بقالُه يوْميْن في العِنايَة المرُكّزة.
أ: يا خبر أبْيَض! أنا مكنْتِش أعْرف. إن شاء الله تِتْطمّنوا عليْه و يْقوم بِالسّلامة.

A: Hey dude, where have you been hiding?
B: I've been in a bad spot for a week now. My dad got really sick, and he's in the ICU now.
A: Oh no! I didn't know. I hope he gets better, and you'll rest assured, God willing.

إن شاء الله can take the place of saying 'yes.'

(in an elevator)

أ: نازِل؟
ب: إن شاء الله.

A: Going down?
B: Yes.

إن شاء الله can also be a way to avoid a direct 'no.' Unfortunately, some people might use it in this sense to avoid giving a direct answer and a commitment.

أ: هتيجي الحفْلة بُكْرة؟
ب: ربِّنا يِسهِّل، إن شاء الله.

A: Are you coming to my party tomorrow?
B: If God makes it possible. God willing!

Run together as if one word, the 'merged' form of إنْشالله (usually followed by بَسّ) is used to beg or urge someone: **at least, even if (just) and usually comes with** بَسّ.

أ: أنا مِش هقْدر آجي معاكُم النّهارْده للأسف.
ب: طب ما تْحاوْلي إنْشالله بسّ نُصّ ساعة!

A: I won't be able to join you today, unfortunately.
B: Come one, try, even if just for half an hour.

The merged إنْشالله **can also express doubt due to obstacles. In this usage, it is interchangeable with** على الله.

أ: حبيبي، مِش هتْوَدّينا مصيف السّنة دي وَلّا أيْه؟
ب: ناوي واللهِ بسّ إنْشالله أعْرف آخُد أجازة بسّ.

A: Honey, aren't you going to take us on a summer trip this year?
B: I intend to, believe me, if only I can get time off from work.

أ: هُوّ قالك إنّه هَيرجّعْلك الفِلوس اللي استلفْها أوّل الشّهْر، مِش كده؟
ب: إنْشالله بسّ يُصَدّق و يِرجّعْها!

A: He told you he'd give you back the money he borrowed next month, right?
B: Let's just hope he keeps his promise and gives it back!

The merged إنْشالله is also used in an angry tone to show resignation or indifference: 'I don't care,' 'let him them do whatever they want.'

أ: خُد بالك لَوْ معزمْتوش بِنِفْسك مُمْكِن مَيحْضَرْش الفرح.

ب: إنْشالله ما حضر الفرح يا عمرّ!

A: Be careful. If you haven't invited him yourself, he might not attend the wedding.

B: I couldn't care less if he attends the wedding, bro!

أ: مِش هتاكْلي؟ إنْتي مكلْتيش حاجة مِر الصّبْح!

ب: لا، مِش هاكُل. مليش نِفْس أطْفح.

أ: خلاص! إنْتي بْتِزْعقي ليْه؟ إنْشالله عنّك ما كلْتي... إنْتي حُرّة!

A: Aren't you going to eat? You haven't eaten anything since this morning!

B: No, I'm not eating. I don't have an appetite to stuff my face.

A: Whatever! Why are you shouting? Don't eat then! As you wish!

طفح is a course slang word for 'to eat.'

ما شاء الله

... and the Evil Eye

العيْن the [evil] eye encompasses the belief that individuals can cause harm by looking at people or things with admiration or envy. To ward off the evil eye when paying someone a compliment or admiring something of theirs, Muslims should add ما شاء الله, literally 'what God has willed.' So, when a Muslim sees that someone has been blessed with something nice, ما شاء الله serves as a self-reminder not to be envious and that all blessings are from God.

It would likely raise eyebrows if a Christian Egyptian or non-Muslim foreigner used this expression. Alternative expressions can be used by anyone (that is, also by non-Muslims) to express congratulations or admiration: a simple !الله, اللّه عليْك, بْراڤو عليْك, or ألْف مبْروك.

أ: ما شاء الله، تبارك الله! العربية شكْلها حِلْو أوي.
ب: ربّنا يِبارِك فيك يا حبيبي. لِسّه جايِبْها إمْبارِح مِن التوْكيل.

A: Mashallah, blessed is God! The car looks really beautiful.
B: Bless you, dear. I just bought it from the dealership.

ما شاء الله God's blessings is synonymous with تبارك الله.

أ: إمْبارِح سامِح و سارة جابوا بنّوتة زيّ القمر سمّوها هناء.

ب: ما شاء الله! ربّنا يِبارِكْلُهُم فيها.

A: Yesterday, Sameh and Sara had a beautiful baby girl that they named Hana.
B: Mashallah! May God bless her for them.

أ: ما شاء الله عليك يا عمْرو! مِحافِظ عَ الرِّياضة كلّ يوْم رغْم كلّ مشاغْلك.

ب: بحاوِل والله.

A: Mashallah, Amr! You keep practicing daily even though you have lots of work.
B: I'm really trying!

أ: رامي عمل أيْه في النّتيجة؟
ب: الحمْدُ لله جاب ٩٥٪ و كِده يقْدر يِدْخُل الكُلِّية اللي عايْزها و هوَّ مِسْتِريّح.
أ: ما شاء الله ربّنا يِوَفّقه و يِحْفظه مِن العيْن.

A: What kind of grade/results did Rami get?
B: Thank God, he got a 95%. Now he can easily enter whichever college he wants.
A: Mashallah! May God grant him success and protect him from the [evil] eye.

ما شاء الله can also be used sarcastically in everyday speech, both by Muslims and non-Muslims. And don't worry. This usage is very casual and won't cause offense.

أ: شُفْتي يا ماما إبْنِك شطّور إزّاي! جِبْت النّهارْده خمْسة و نُصّ مِن عشرة في الكُوِيز.

ب: يا ما شاء الله! يا فرْحِتي بيك يا خويا!

A: Mom, look what a cute, hardworking boy your son is! I got 5.5 out of 10 on today's quiz.
B: [sarcastically] Oh wow! I'm so happy with you, boy!

الحَمْدُ لِلَّه

Praise be to God!

الحَمْدُ لِلَّه **is an expression of gratitude to God:** All praise is due to God.

أ: طَمِّنّي العملية نِجْحِت؟

ب: الحَمْدُ لِلَّه! بابا طِلِع مِنْها و في العِنايَة دِلْوَقْتي.

أ: ألف حَمْد و شُكْر ليك يا ربّ!

A: Tell me, was the operation successful?
B: [Yes.] Thank God! Dad is out of surgery and is in the ICU now.
A: A thousand praises and thanks to You, Lord!

People also use الحَمْدُ لِلَّه **as a response to an inquiry on their well-being, whether they are doing great or not. You can sense the intended meaning according to the tone.**

To express that you are happy, enthusiastic, or grateful:

أ: كامِل، إزَّيِّك؟

ب: عُمر! أنا تمام الحمْدُ لِلّه. إنْتَ أخْبارك؟

أ: أنا تمام. قولّي عملْت أيْه في الامْتِحان إمْبارِح؟

ب: الحمْدُ لِلّه! تقْريباً قفلْته.

A: Kamel, how are you?
B: Omar! I'm fine, thank God. What about you?
A: I'm good. Tell me, how did you do on the exam yesterday?
B: Thank God! I nearly got a perfect score.

قفّل [lit. to lock] to get full marks, 100% (on a test)

To express a neutral tone (neither especially happy nor sad):

أ: و أخْبار الشُّغْل الجِديد معاكي أيْه؟

ب: الحمْدُ لِلّه ماشي الحال... دعْواتك.

A: And how's the new job going for you?
B: Thank God, it's all right. Pray for me.

(two friends at a coffee house)

أ: مِش ناوي تْبطّل تدْخين بقى؟ عميتْني يا عمر!

ب: والله الحمْدُ لِلّه بطّلت سجايِر بسّ لِسّه الشّيشة. دعْواتك بقى ربّنا يْتوب عليّا مِنْها.

A: Aren't you willing to quit smoking? You blinded me [with your smoke], bro!
B: Thank God, I really did quit cigarettes, but not the shisha [hookah, water pipe] yet. Pray for me that God may help me to give it up.

To express that you are not happy but grateful to God all the same:

أ: أخْبارك أيْه يا حبيبْتي؟
ب: الحمْدُ لِلّه. زيّ ما إنْتي شايْفة...

A: How are you doing, darling?
B: Thank God. As you can see...

أ: و عملْت أيْه بعْد ما العقْد اتْفسخ؟
ب: والله آديني قدّمْت في كذا مكان و عنْدي إنْتِرْڤْيو السّبْت اللي جايّ. بسّ الحمْدُ لِلّه على كُلّ حال.

A: So, what did you do after your contract was canceled?
B: Well, here I am. I applied to a couple of places, and I have an interview next Saturday... but Thank God in any case.

To express relief:

أ: ها لِحِقْت تْجيب تذْكرة قبْل الشّبّاك ما يِقْفِل؟
ب: كانوا آخِر اتْنيْن و لِحِقْتُهُم!
أ: الحمْدُ لِلّه! كِده هنِلْحق نوْصل إسْكِنْدِرية قبْل المعاد كمان.

A: So, were you able to get a [train/bus] ticket before the window closed?
B: These were the last two... and I got them!
A: Thank God! So, we'll be able to reach Alexandria in time for our appointment.

Some synonymous, interchangeable expressions use the word حمْد **praise.**

أ: و أخْبارك أيْه دلْوَقْتي بعْد ما رجعْت؟
ب: الحمْد و الشُّكْر لله! كلُّه تمام.

A: And how are you doing now since you've come back?
B: Praise and thanks be to God! Everything's fine.

أ: بسّ أنا حاسّك بقيْت أحْسن بعْد ما نقلْت إسْكنْدرية.
ب: فعْلاً والله. أنا نفْسيّتي هنا أحْسن كتير.
أ: المهمّ أحْوالك كلّها تمام؟
ب: يسْتاهل الحمْد. كلُّه زيّ الفلّ.

A: But I feel you're doing better since you've moved to Alexandria.
B: Yes, true. I feel much better here.
A: And more importantly, is your overall situation good?
B: He [God] deserves praise. Everything is perfect.

زيّ الفلّ [lit. like a jasmine flower] lovely, in perfect condition

A related expression الشُّكْر لله the thanks is for [due to] God **can be used as a response to a thank-you. It literally means that the thanks should belong to God (and not to me).**

(in a taxi)

أ: ماشي أنا هنْزل هنا إن شاء الله. متْشكّرة جدّاً.
ب: الشُّكْر لله يا مدام... حمْدلله ع السّلامة.

A: Okay, I'll get out here. Thanks so much.
B: The thanks belong to God [that you arrived safely], ma'am.

The expression حَمْدُ لِلّه عَ السَّلامة is derived from الحَمْدُ لِلّه and literally means 'thank God that you arrived safely.' It sometimes takes a pronoun depending on the person being spoken to: على سلامتْكُم/سلامتك/سلامتك.

أ: وَصلْتي مصْر إمْتى؟

ب: لِسّه واصْلة المطار إمْبارِح.

أ: حمدْلله على سلامتِك حبيبْتي!

A: When did you arrive in Egypt?
B: I just arrived at the airport yesterday.
A: Thank God you're back safe, honey!

أ: مين جِهْ؟

ب: أنا يا ماما. أخدْت إذْن و مْشيت بدْري النّهارْده مِن الشُّغْل.

أ: حمدْلله على سلامتِك يا حبيبي. تِتْغدّى؟

A: Who is it?
B: It's me, Mom! I got off work early today.
A: Welcome back home, honey. You want lunch?

أ: ألو؟ إزّيّك يا مْحمّد؟ طمّنّي بابا طِلع مِن المُسْتشْفى؟

ب: آه يا طنْط الحمْدُ لِلّه طِلع إمْبارِح.

أ: حمدْلله على سلامتُه حبيبي. سلِّمْلي عليْه كِتير و قوليّ أقْدر آجي أزورُه إمْتى؟

A: Hello? Mohamed, how are you? Give me an update. Did [your] father get out of the hospital?
B: Yes, auntie! Thank God, he was released yesterday.
A: Thank God he's out safe, dear. Extend my greetings to him, and let me know when I can come visit him.

(on a long train journey)

أ: هُوَّ إحْنا كِده وِصِلْنا الأقْصُر؟

ب: آه خلاص. حمْدِلله ع السّلامة.

A: Have we arrived in Luxor yet?
B: Yes, [we have] already. Thank God for the safe arrival.

التَّوَكُّل على الله

Reliance on God

A well-known saying of the Prophet is اعْقِلْها وتَوَكَّل (Tether it [the camel] and trust in God.), **which is to say** 'Depend on God, but also do your part.' التَّوَكُّل على الله is an Islamic concept and teaching about maintaining a balance between trust in God while still actively doing your part. The verb form اِتْوَكَّل is used in some expressions.

As a set expression, the perfect-tense تَوَكَّلْت borrowing from Modern Standard Arabic followed by على الله shows intention but with an acknowledgment that the outcome depends on God's will.

أ: عايِز أشْتِـري العربية اللي شُفْناها إمْبارِح.
ب: قرار كُوَيِّس... العربية دي لُقْطة فِعْلاً.
أ: خلاص تَوَكَّلْت على الله.

A: I want to buy that car we saw yesterday.
B: Good decision! That car's a great deal.
A: I depend on God.

As an imperative of the verb اِتْوَكِّل (the Egyptian equivalent of the Modern Standard Arabic verb تَوَكِّل) followed by على الله means 'Go for it' / 'Go ahead.'

أ: ماما، أنا عايِز أَتْقدِّم لِنجْلاء بِنْت عمِّي. أيْه رأيِك؟
ب: اِتْوَكِّل على الله يابْني. مِش هتْلاقي أحْسن مِنها.

A: Mom, I want to propose to my cousin Naglaa. What's your opinion?
B: Go for it, son! You won't find anyone better than her.

The imperative اِتْوَكِّل (and its more colloquial variant اِتِّكِّل) can also be used to bid someone farewell. على الله can be omitted in this sense.

أ: السّاعة بقِت ١٢. لازِم أمْشي.
ب: طب اِتْوَكِّلي (على الله) و طمِّنينا لمّا توْصلي.

A: It's twelve o'clock now. I have to take off.
B: Okay, bye-bye, and let us know when you arrive.

أ: يَلّا بينا!
ب: أنا هعْقُد كمان شُوَيَّة. اِتِّكِّل إنْتَ على الله!

A: Let's go!
B: I'm going to stay a bit longer. You go ahead and take off.

أ: طيِّب أيْه كِده؟ خلاص؟ مِش هتِحْتاجونا في حاجة؟
ب: لا خلاص. اِتِّكِّلوا إنْتو بقى.

A: So then? All done? You need us for anything?
B: Nope. You guys can take off now.

Likewise, these verbs can be used in the first person as a bare imperfect (أَتْوَكِّل) أَتَّكِل or future-tense verb هَتِّكِل to take leave.

أ: هَقوم أنا. أَتَّكِل على الله.
ب: معَ السَّلامة.

A: I'm going now.
B: Goodbye!

أ: مِش هَتِتْغدّى معانا؟
ب: لا يا دوْب أَتَّكِل (على الله) أنا بقى علشان ألْحق الماتْش.

A: Won't you have lunch with us?
B: No, it's about time I leave so I can catch the game.

ربّنا يْسهّل

May God make it easy!

ربّنا يْسهّل literally means 'May our Lord make [it] easy.' Its usage is similar to إن شاء الله to express willingness or hope about the future and is often used as a response to plans, requests and so on. It may express a sincere willingness "I hope so" or as a non-committal way to end a discussion: We'll see about this [later or never].

أ: مِش هنْوَدّي العربية تِتْصلّح؟
ب: ربّنا يْسهّل إن شاء الله. أقْبض بسّ أوِّل الشّهْر و أصلّحْها على طول.

A: Aren't we going to take the car in for repairs?
B: I hope so, God willing. Just let me get paid at the beginning of the month, and then I'll get it fixed straight away.

أ: ماما، مُمْكِن بعْد الامْتِحانات أسافِر معَ صْحابي شرْمٍ؟
ب: ربِّنا يْسهِّل... لمّا تْخلّص نِبْقى نْشوف.

A: Mom, can I travel with my friends to Sharm El-Sheikh after the exams?
B: We'll see... When you're done, we can see.

ربّنا ياخْدك

Damn you!

ربّنا ياخْدك literally means 'May our Lord take you,' that is, your soul. It's a statement used in anger, a prayer wishing someone dead.

أ: روح يا شيْخ، ربّنا ياخْدك!
ب: يا ريْت علشان أرْتاح مِن خِلْقِتك!

A: Get out of here, man! May God take your soul!
B: I wish... at least I wouldn't have to see your ugly face!

ارْتاح مِن to find rest from [the absence of]
خِلْقة impolite slang for 'face': ugly face, mug

The expression can also be used in the third person to express hatred or despisal.

أ: شُفْت الحَيوان ده عمل أيْه في مْراتُه و عْيالُه؟
ب: عرِفْت، آه. ربّنا ياخْدُه! ده مِش بني آدم!

A: Did you hear what this savage did to his wife and kids?
B: Yeah, I heard. May God take his soul. He's not human!

ربّنا يِكْرِمك

May God be generous with you!

ربّنا يِكْرِمك (lit. may our Lord be generous with you) and ربّنا يْخلّيك (lit. may our Lord keep you (safe)) are used interchangeably to express appreciation. Both expressions can be used when making a request or as a thank-you.

أ: أنا خلاص ظبطْتِلك الحجْز بتاع القطْر بُكْره.
ب: ربّنا يِكْرِمك حبيبي! مُتْشكِّر جِدّاً.

A: I've made the reservation for the train tomorrow.
B: Bless you, dear! Thank you so much.

أ: ربّنا يْخلّيك، مُمْكِن تِنزِّلي الشُّنط للعربية؟
ب: حاضِر يافنْدِم، أوْمُري.

A: Bless you, would you please take these suitcases down to the car?
B: Right away, ma'am. At your service.

Section 6

hand

Body parts appear in so many idioms and proverbs in Egyptian Arabic. In this section, we'll take a special look at the word إيد hand, which is particularly interesting. Its metaphorical senses are similar to those of 'hand' in English, expressing character traits, human behavior, and actions (after all, we do so many things with our hands), assistance, accessibility (being within reach), among others.

track 078	page 186	light-handed	إيده خفيفة
track 079	page 188	heavy-handed	إيده تقيلة
track 080	page 189	deaf-handed	إيده طرشا
track 081	page 190	long-handed	إيده طويلة
track 082	page 191	dry-handed	إيده ناشفة
track 083	page 192	pierced-handed	إيده مخرومة
track 084	page 193	loose-handed	إيده سايبة

track 085	page 195	Be frugal!	اِمْسِك إيدَك!
track 086	page 197	as he witnessed...	على إيدُه
track 087	page 199	Stop here!	على إيدَك
track 088	page 200	I support you	إيدي على كِتْفَك
track 089	page 201	to extend one's hand	مَدَّ إيدُه
track 090	page 203	out of reach	العين بصيرة و الإيد قصيرة
track 091	page 205	to have a good grip on someone	مِسكه من إيدُه اللي بتوجعه
track 092	page 206	to be right under one's nose	تحت إيدُه
track 093	page 207	May your hands be safe!	تِسلم إيدَك
track 094	page 208	to kiss one's hand	باس إيدُه
track 095	page 209	Gasp!	كُنْت حاطِط إيدي على قلْبي
track 096	page 211	to ask for one's hand in marriage	طلب إيدُها
track 097	page 212	A single hand cannot clap.	إيد لوَحْدها متسقَّفش
track 098	page 213	a hand upon a hand	إيد على إيد تِساعِد

track 099	page 214	to lift one's hand from	شال إيدُه مِن
track 100	page 216	The answer's right in front of you.	الحلّ في إيدُه
track 101	page 217	generous	اللي في إيدُه مِش لُه
track 102	page 218	a lost cause	إيدك مِنُّه و الأرْض
track 103	page 220	I'm game!	أنا مِن إيدك دي لإيدك دي
track 104	page 221	Hey, watch it!	لمّ إيدك و لُسانك
track 105	page 223	essential	إيدي و رِجْلي
track 106	page 225	to come back empty-handed	إيد وَرا و إيد قُدّام
track 107	page 227	How was I supposed to know?	هشِمّ على ضهْر إيدي
track 108	page 229	to wait and watch	وقِف على إيدُه
track 109	page 231	You don't get it!	اللي إيدُه في المايّة...
track 110	page 233	Idle hands are the devil's tool.	الإيد البطّالة نِجْسة

إيدُه خفيفة

light-handed

إيدُه خفيفة [lit. one's hand is light] has two basic meanings. First, it can describe someone who has a gentle touch and doesn't cause pain.

(an elderly patient to her doctor)

أ: إيدك خفيفة يابْني. الحُقْنة مَوجَعِتْنيش.

ب: بِالشِّفا يا حاجّة.

A: You have a gentle touch, young man! The shot didn't hurt at all.
B: Get well soon, hajja.

It can also be used with a completely different meaning with a negative connotation to describe a thief who has agile hands.

أ: شُفْت اللي حصلِّي الصُّبْح؟

ب: خيرْ؟

أ: الواد إيدُه خفيفة بِشكْل قال أيْه بِيْبيعْلي مناديل و في ثانْيَة خد الموبايْل و فصّ مِلْح و داب!

A: Do you know what happened to me this morning?
B: What?
A: A boy whose hands were so quick pretended to sell me tissues, took my cell phone in a second, and was gone like that!

* فصّ ملْح و داب idiom [lit. a pinch of salt and melted] to vanish into thin air

إيْدُه تْقيلة

heavy-handed

إيْدُه تْقيلة [lit. one's hand is heavy] implies that someone (a nurse giving an injection, etc.) does not have a gentle touch. (It differs from the English expression 'heavy-handed' as it does not mean clumsy or oppressive.)

أ: أنا تعْبانة جِدّاً النّهارْده و حاسّة إنّي دايِسْني قطْر.
ب: ليْه بسّ؟ حصل أيْه؟
أ: إمْبارِح رُحْت جلْسِةْ مساچ بسّ البِنْت إيديْها كانِت تِقيلة جِدّاً.

A: I don't feel good today. I feel like I've been hit by a train.
B: Why? What happened?
A: Yesterday, I had a massage, but the girl pressed on me too hard.

إيدُه طرْشا

deaf-handed

إيدُه طرْشا [lit. one's hand is deaf] **is used to describe someone who can hit with force.**

أ: إمْبارِح ماجِد مِسِك صاحْبُه عدمُه العافْيَة.
ب: فظيع ماجِد! ده إيدُه طرْشا!

A: Yesterday, Maged grabbed his friend and beat him up.
B: Maged is horrible! He can really pack a punch!

إيدُه طَويلة

long-handed

إيدُه طَويلة [lit. one's hand is long] describes someone who is prone to theft.

أ: أنا مشّيْت الصّنايعي اللي كان بِيبيِّض الشّقّة.
ب: ليْه؟
أ: إيدُه طَويلة. كُلّ شْوَيّة ألاقي حاجة ناقْصة.

A: I let go of the worker who was painting my apartment.
B: Why?
A: He had sticky fingers. Every now and then, I would find something missing.

إيدُه ناشْفة

dry-handed

إيدُه ناشْفة [lit. one's hand is dry] describes someone who is miserly or stingy with money.

أ: جِهاز الكُمْبيوتر ده قديم جِدًّا و مِش نافِع خالِص.
ب: هنعْمِل أيْه ما إنْتَ عارِف صاحِب الشِّرْكة إيدُه ناشْفة، مفيش فايْدة فيه!

A: This computer is too old and not working anymore.
B: What can we do? You know the owner of the company is a tight-fisted hopeless cause [who won't be willing to buy new computers].

إيدُه مخْرومة

pierced-handed

إيدُه مخْرومة [lit. one's hand is pierced (has a hole in it)] describes someone who spends a lot of money without control.

أ: بابا لَو سمحْت، عايِز ميةْ جِنيْهْ علشان أشْتِري كُتُب للكلّية.

ب: أنا مِش لِسّا مدّيك ٣٠٠ مِن يوْمينْ؟

أ: لا، ما هُمّا خِلْصوا في مُواصْلات و شحْن موبايْل.

ب: إنتَ أيْه يابْني؟ إيدك مخْرومة! ما تِمْسِك إيدك شُويّة!

A: Dad, please, I want 100 LE to buy some books for college.
B: Didn't I just give you 300 two days ago?
A: That's already gone, spent on transportation and cellphone reloading [of prepaid units].
B: What's the matter with you, son? Does your hand have a hole in it? Hold onto your money more!

إيدُه سايْبة

loose-handed

إيدُه سايْبة [lit. one's hand is loose] **has two meanings.**

It can be synonymous with إيدُه مخْرومة, **implying a loose hand cannot hold onto money.**

أ: الله! حِلْوَة أوي الشَّنْطة دي! جِبْتيها بْكام يا حبيبْتي؟
ب: جِبْتها بـ سُتّْميةْ جِنيْهْ يا ماما.
أ: يا بِنْتي، إنْتي إيدِك سايْبة كِده ليْه؟ هتِفْتِحي بيْت إزّاي، نِفْسي أعْرف!

A: Wow! This is a very nice purse. How much did you get it for, dear?
B: I got it for 600 LE, Mom.
A: Why is your hand so loose, girl? How will you ever establish a home? I'd like to know! [that is, manage a household as a housewife]

It can also be used more literally to mean someone who is clumsy and drops things.

أ: حمادة، مُمْكِن تِدّي الطّبق ده لِبابا؟

ب: ... ماما، الطّبق وِقِع مِن إيدي على السّجادة!

أ: يا نْهار أبْيَض! إنْتَ إيدك سايْبة كِده ليْه؟ ماسِك ديْل قُطّة؟ ما تمْسِك الحاجة كْوَيِّس!

A: Hamada, could you please give this plate to your dad?
B: ... Mom, the plate has fallen out of my hand onto the carpet!
A: Oh my! Why is your hand that loose? Are you holding a cat's tail? Hold on to things better!

ماسِك ديْل قُطّة؟ [lit. (are you) holding a cat's tail?] is a common rebuke to someone who has clumsily dropped something.

امْسِك إيدك!

Be frugal!

مِسِك إيدُه (or لَمّ إيدُه) [lit. to hold (back) one's own hand] implies that one should be more frugal–tighten the purse strings a bit. It is often used in the imperative.

أ: باقي قدّ أيْه في مصْروف البيْت؟
ب: حَوالي ألْف و سُبْعْميةْ جِنيْه.
أ: يا نْهار أبْيَض! ده لِسّه باقي نصّ الشّهْر. لازِم نِمْسِك إيديْنا شْوَيّة.

A: How much is left in the household budget?
B: Around 1700 LE.
A: Oh my! And we still have half of the month left. We have to tighten our purse strings a bit.

أ: ماما عايِز ٥٠ جِنيْهْ علشانْ نازِل.
ب: أنا مِش لِسّه مِدّيّاك فِلوس إمْبارِح؟

أ: ما أنا صرفْتُهُم كُلُّهُم إمْبارِح و متبْقاش مِنْهُم حاجة.

ب: يابْني لِمّ إيدك شُوَيّة في المصاريف. مِش هيِنْفع كِده!

A: Mom, I need 50 LE because I'm going out.
B: Didn't I just give you money yesterday?
A: I spent it all, and there's nothing left.
B: Son, rein in your spending a bit. It's not going to work this way!

على إيدُه

as he witnessed...

على إيدُه [lit. to one's hand] is used to emphasize that someone has first-hand knowledge of something–that they have witnessed it personally and can attest to it.

أ: احْكيلُه يا نُهى، الرّاجِل قالّنا أيْه.
ب: على إيدي، رفض تماماً يِنزِّل في السِّعْر.

A: Noha, tell him what the man said to us.
B: [I was there, and he said that...] he absolutely refused to lower the price.

The expression can also be used in the second or third person.

على إيدِك، الرّاجِل رفض يِنزِّل في السِّعْر. المَوْضوع كان قُدّامِك!

You saw yourself that the man refused to lower the price. It happened right in front of you!

اِسْأل حُسام، على إيدُه، الرّاجِل قُدّامُه رفض يِنزِّل في السِّعْر.

Ask Hossam. He was there and saw how the man wouldn't go down on the price.

اِسْأل نَوال، على إيدْها، الرّاجِل قُدّامْها رفض يِنزِّل في السِّعْر.

Ask Nawal. She was there and saw how the man wouldn't go down on the price.

A variation is to use the Modern Standard Arabic word يَد instead of إيد: على يَدّي, على يَدّك, على يَدُّه, على يَدُّه, etc.

أ: سِمِعْت إنّ سارة عايْزة تتْطلّق مِن علي. مفيش أيّ سبيل للصُّلْح؟
ب: أنا رُحْتِلْها مع حُسام و على يَدُّه رفضِت أيّ مُحاوَلة للصُّلْح. حتّى اسْأله.
أ: لا، صادِق... بسّ كْوَيِّس إنَّكُم حاوِلْتوا تْصلَّحوا. ربِّنا يكْتبْلُهُم الخيْر.

A: I heard Sara wants to divorce Ali. Is there no room for reconciliation?
B: I went to her with Hossam, and [he witnessed that] she refused a hearing for conciliation. You can even ask him.
A: I believe you. It's good you tried, at least. May God destine what is good for them.

على إيدك

Stop here!

In the previous section, we saw that على إيدك can emphasize that 'you' witnessed something. But it has another meaning and use. على إيدك is how you can tell your taxi driver that you have arrived at your destination and you want him to pull over and let you out. It is synonymous with على جمْب.

أ: على إيدك. هِنا يا أُسْطى.
ب: نازْلة يا مدام؟
أ: أَيْوَه.

A: Stop here, sir.
B: You want to get out here, ma'am?
A: Yes.

إيدي على كِتْفك

I support you

إيدي على كِتْفك [lit. my hand is on your shoulder] expresses support for someone's idea or proposal.

أ: أنا نِفْسي أوي نِبْدأ مشْروعْنا الخاصّ.
ب: إيدي على كِتْفك!

A: I really want to start our own business.
B: I'm all for that!

مدّ إيدُه

to extend one's hand

مدّ إيدُه [lit. to extend one's hand] **has three meanings, depending on the context.**

In the context of food, it is used in the imperative to encourage guests to help themselves.

أ: أيْه الأكْل ده كُلّه؟ تِسْلم إيديكي!
ب: بِالهنا و الشِّفا! يَلّا مِدّوا إيديكو، متِتْكِسْفوش.

A: Wow! What's all this food? Bless your hands!
B: Bon appetit! Come on and eat! Don't be shy.

When followed by the preposition على and a person, it means to hit.

أ: ماما، زيْن خبطْني في كِتْفي جامِد!
ب: وَلد! إيّاك تِمدّ إيدك على أُخْتك تاني! إنْتَ فاهِم؟

A: Mom! Zain hit me hard in the shoulder!
B: Boy, don't you ever raise your hand against your sister again! Do you hear me?

201 | TALK LIKE AN EGYPTIAN

When على is followed by a thing, it means to steal.

أ: أنا مِش مِرْتاحة لِلسِّتّ اللي بْتيجي تْنضّف لِماما.

ب: مدِّت إيديْها على حاجة؟

أ: لأ حرام! هِيَّ أمينة بسّ شُغْلها بقى أيّ كلام.

A: I'm not comfortable with the lady who comes and cleans the house for mom.
B: Did she steal anything?
A: No, God forbid! She's an honest woman, but her work is not really that good anymore.

العيْن بصيرة و الإيد قصيرة

out of reach

العيْن بصيرة و الإيد قصيرة [lit. The eye sees, but the hand is short.] is a common proverb that expresses that something is unfortunately out of one's reach or unaffordable.

أ: مِش ناوي تِتْقدّم لِمها بقى؟

ب: العيْن بصيرة و الإيد قصيرة... حاوِلْت و أهْلها رفضوا.

أ: طب ما تْحاوِل تاني. متِعرْفْش ربِّنا مْقدّر أيْه.

A: Aren't you going to propose to Maha?
B: It's not going to happen. I already tried, but her family refused.
A: Then try again. You never know what God has destined.

أ: مِش ناوي تْجيبْلك عربية بقى يابْني؟
ب: والله العينْ بصيرة و الإيد قصيرة.
أ: ربِّنا يُرْزُقك إن شاء الله.

A: Aren't you going to get yourself a car, man?
B: I really wish I could, but I simply can't afford to.
A: Hopefully, God will provide for you.

مِسكُه مِن إيدُه اللي بْتِوْجَعُه

to have a good grip on someone

مِسكُه مِن إيدُه اللي بْتِوْجَعُه [lit. to hold one by his hand that hurts] is a rather straightforward metaphor meaning to take advantage of someone's weakness.

أ: إنْتَ أيْه اللي مُخَلّيك مِسْتحْمِل كُلّ ده؟ ما تْسيب الشُّغْل!

ب: ما هُوَّ ماسِكْني مِن إيدي اللي بْتِوْجَعْني. هُوَّ عارِف إنّي مِحْتاج للشُّغْل جِدّاً الفترة دي.

A: What's making you put up with all of this? Just quit!
B: He's got a good grip on me. He knows I really need this job right now.

تحْت إيدُه

to be right under one's nose

تحْت إيدُه [lit. under one's hand] means that something is readily accessible–close at hand.

أ: حدّ شاف نضّارْتي يا جماعة؟ كانِت تحْت إيدي حالاً.

ب: ما إنْتَ لابِسْها يابْني! اللي واخِد عقْلك!

A: Has anyone seen my glasses? They were just here!
B: You're wearing them, man! Hello?!

اللي واخِد عقْلك [lit. who's taken your mind]

تِسْلم إيدك

May your hands be safe!

تِسْلم إيدك and تِسْلم إيديك [lit. may your hand(s) be safe] is used to thank someone who has done or made something for you with their own hands. It is most commonly used to express gratitude to someone who has prepared a meal.

أ: أيْه رأيُك في الأكْل يا حبيبي؟
ب: تُحْفة! تِسْلم إيديكي.

A: What do you think of the food, honey?
B: It's amazing! Compliments to the chef!

أ: خلاص أنا صلّحْت الحنفية يا مدام. كِده مِش هتْنقّط تاني.
ب: تِسْلم إيدك... حِسابك كام بقى؟

A: Okay, I've fixed the faucet, ma'am. It won't be dripping anymore.
B: Thank you! How much do I owe you?

باس إيدُه

to kiss one's hand

[lit. to kiss one's hand] is an idiom meaning to beg, implore.

أ: لِعِلْمك محمّد باس إيدي عشان مسيبْش الشُّغْل معاه بسّ أنا فِعْلاً خلاص جِبْت أخْري.

ب: طب و هتِعْمِل أيْه؟

أ: هكمِّل معاه شهْر كمان و بعْدين هسيب.

A: For your information, Mohamed begged me not to quit [working with him], but I've had enough, really.
B: Well, what are you going to do?
A: I'll stay on for another month, then leave.

أ: ده كان هَيْبوس إيدي علشان أشْتِري العربية منُّه.

ب: و اِشْتِريتْها؟

أ: لأ طبْعاً... مكُنْتِش عايز أشْتِريها أساساً.

A: He was practically begging me to buy the car from him.
B: And did you buy it?
A: Of course not! I didn't want to buy it in the first place.

كُنْت حاطِط إيدي على قلْبي

Gasp!

[كُنْت حاطِط إيدي على قلْبي **lit.** I was putting my hand on my heart] expresses extreme worry or thrill and anticipation that something vital will happen.

أ: إمْبارِح لمّا جِهْ جوْن الكونْغو، كُنّا حاطّين إيدينا على قلْبِنا.

ب: بسّ الحمْدُ لِلّه محمّد صلاح بلّ ريقْنا في آخِر لحْظة و جاب جوْن.

A: Yesterday, when the Congo [team] made a goal, our hearts dropped.

B: Thank God that Mohamed Salah saved us at the last moment and scored a goal!

Notice that the plural variation is used in the dialogue: كُنَّا حاطّين إيدينا على قلْبِنا.

بلّ ريقُه [lit. to moisten one's saliva] means to quench one's thirst, and here it is used metaphorically to show that Salah provided feelings of relief, gratitude, and joy to anxious fans.

طلب إيْدها

to ask for one's hand in marriage

طلب إيْدها [lit. to ask for one's hand] means to ask permission to marry one's daughter (niece, etc.) as per the Egyptian custom.

أ: اِسْمحْلي يا عمّو أنول الشّرف و أطْلُب إيد بِنْت حضْرتك.

ب: الشّرف لينا يابْني بسّ طبْعاً الرّأي رأيُها.

A: Allow me, sir, to have the honor and ask for your daughter's hand in marriage.
B: The honor is ours, son, but of course, it's up to her.

إيد لِوَحْدها متْسقّفْش

A single hand cannot clap.

إيد لِوَحْدها متْسقّفْش [lit. a single hand cannot clap] is a proverb that expresses the value of cooperation and unity. It takes two hands to clap.

أ: أنا بفكّر أسيبهُم في مشروع التّخرُّج و أعْمِل حاجة لِوَحْدي.
ب: إيد لِوَحْدها متْسقّفْش يا بِنْتي. خلّيكي مع زمايلِك أحْسن.

A: I'm considering leaving the graduation project group to work on my own.
B: A single hand cannot clap, daughter. You'd better stick with your classmates.

A مشروع التّخرُّج graduation project is required for some degrees. Engineering students prepare a proposal project with a demonstration and presentation. It is then evaluated by the professor, and the whole team gets the same grade. In more theoretical fields, it might be a mini-thesis, research project, or for translation students, a translation project.

إيد على إيد تِساعِد

a hand upon a hand

(إيد على إيد (تِساعِد)) [lit. a hand upon a hand (helps)] has a similar sentiment to the proverb إيد لِوَحْدها متْسقّفْش (of the previous segment) to encourage a spirit of cooperation.

أ: حدّ يِقوم يِساعِد ماما في الأكْل.
ب: حاضِر يا بابا، ما تيجي معانا إنْتَ كمان؟
أ: يَلّا بينا، إيد على إيد!

A: Somebody, get up and help mom with the food.
B: Okay, Dad! Why don't you come, too?
A: Okay, let's do it. A hand upon hand!

شال إيدُه مِن

to lift one's hand from

شال إيدُه مِن [lit. to lift one's hand from] **implies that someone is stepping back so as not to interfere, but it can sometimes have a negative connotation, as in the second example.**

In a neutral connotation, it means to mind one's own business by leaving a matter alone.

أ: ما تُحاوِل تِلاقي لِمَحْمود أيّ شُغْل.
ب: والله أنا كُلّ ما أقولُّه على شُغْل يِطلّعْلي فيه القُطط الفاطْسة فا أنا شِلْت إيدي مِن المَوْضوع.
كُلّ واحِد عارِف مَصْلحْتُه. و هُوَّ لازِم يِدوَّر بِنفْسُه.

A: Could you try to find a job for Mahmoud?
B: Whenever I tell him about a job, he just goes on about its cons. So, I just lifted my hand from this issue. Everyone knows what's best for himself. He'll have to look [for a job] himself.

طلّع فيه القُطط الفاطْسة [lit. to claim it has dead cats in it] means to find a reason to refuse something.

It can also be an accusation of being irresponsible by not being more involved.

(A couple whose son's school wants them to come in for a meeting.)

أ: شُفْتي؟ الوَلد جايْله اِسْتِدْعا وَليّ أَمْر.

ب: يا ما شاء الله! طيِّب روح إنْتَ معاه المدْرسة بُكره

أ: يا سلام! و إنْتي هتْشيلي إيدِك مِن القِصّة كِده؟ أنا وَرايا شُغْل. هروح إزاي؟

ب: أنا طول السَّنة صوْتي اتْبح و أنا بقولَّك الوَلد مُهْمِل في مُذاكْرِته و إنْتَ حاطِط إيدك في المايَّة البارْدة.

A: Did you see? The boy's got a parent-teacher meeting.
B: (sarcastically) Oh, great! Okay, go with him to the school tomorrow.
A: Seriously? And you'll simply lift your hand from the whole thing just like that! I have work tomorrow. How am I going to go?
B: I've lost my voice [from repeating myself over and over] all year telling you the boy is paying no attention to his studies while you just couldn't care less.

حطّ إيدُه في المايَّة البارْدة [lit. *to put one's hand in cold water*] is an idiom that means 'to act *indifferent*', '*be detached and unconcerned*'.

الحلّ في إيدُه

The answer's right in front of you.

الحلّ في إيدُه [lit. the solution is in one's hand] **makes use of the metaphor** 'in one's hand' **to mean** present, easily accessible, right in front of one.

أ: كريم مزْنوق جِدّاً الفتْرة دي و كان مِش عارِف يِتْصرّف إزّاي.

ب: واللهِ الحلّ في إيده. يِبِيع العربية و يْفكّ زنْقتُه وقُدّام يِبْقى يِجيبْلُه واحْدة تانْيَة على قدّ الحال.

A: Kareem is tight on money now and has no idea how he'll manage.
B: The solution is right in front of him. He can sell his car and fix his tight situation. Then, later on, he can get another one that fits his circumstances.

اللي في إيدُه مِش لُه

generous

اللي في إيدُه مِش لُه/ليه [lit. what is in one's hand is not his] implies that someone is **extremely generous, giving whatever he has (in his hand) away.**

أ: شُفْتي عمّو محمود إمْبارِح و أنا بقولُّه "حِلْوَة أوي السّاعة اللي في إيدك." راح قلعْها و إدّاهالي! بِجدّ أنا مبحبِّش حدّ في العيْلة دي قدُّه!

ب: محْمود ده طول عُمْرُه مفيش أطْيَب منُّه و اللي في إيدُه مِش ليه.

أ: ربِّنا يِكْرمُه يا ربّ.

A: Did you see Uncle Mahmoud yesterday when I told him, "The watch in your hand is really nice," and he took it off and gave it to me! Seriously, I love no one in this entire family more than him!

B: Mahmoud has always been the kindest, and he is extremely giving.

A: May God be generous toward him.

إيدك مِنُّه و الأرْض

a lost cause

إيدك مِنُّه و الأرْض [lit. your hand from him and the ground] means that your hand will be at the same level as the ground. It implies that someone is useless, a lost cause. إيدك and مِنُّه change form depending on the addressee and referent, respectively.

أ: أنا مِحْتاج حدّ معايا الأسْبوع الجايّ و أنا بنْقُل
ب: طب ما تْقول لِكَريم يِيجي يُظْبُط الدُّنْيا معاك.
أ: لا كَريم مين! ده إيدك مِنُّه والأرْض. هَييجيلي بعْد الهنا بْسنة لمّا أكون خلّصْت أساساً.

A: I need someone [to help me] next week while I'm moving.
B: Why don't you ask Kareem to come over and help you with stuff?
A: Kareem who? He's a hopeless cause. He'll just come after the whole thing is over when I'm already done with everything.

بَعْد الهنا بْسنة [lit. a year after the well-being] too late, after the appropriate time

أ: يا نْهار أبْيَض! الشّنْطة سوسِتْها اتْقطعِت.
ب: طب ورّيها لِسلْوى كِده يِمْكِن تِعْرف تصلّحْها.
أ: سلْوى دي إيدِك مِنْها و الأرْض. دي مبْتِعْرفْش تْخيّط زُرار!

A: Oh my! The purse's zipper has come off.
B: Well, show it to Salwa. Maybe she can fix it.
A: Salwa's useless. She can't even sew a button.

أ: لَوْ تعْبانة قولي لِلولاد يِروّقوا البيْت.
ب: محدِّش مِنْهُم بِيْساعِدْني! إيدك مِنْهُم والأرْض!

A: If you're tired, tell the kids to clean up the house.
B: None of them helps me! They're a lost cause.

أنا مِن إيدك دي لإيدك دي

I'm game!

أنا مِن إيدك دي لإيدك دي [lit. I'm from your hand to the other] means that I am willing to do whatever you want. I'm game.; I'm all in.

أ: أنا بِجِدّ اِتْخنقْت. نِفْسي نْسافِر نْغيّر جوّ يوْمين في أيّ حِتّة.

ب: أنا مِن إيدِك دي لإيدِك دي! اِنْويها بسّ و قوليلي.

أ: خلاص ناخُد أجازة الخميس و نْسافِر مِن الأربع باللّيْل.

ب: حِلْو أوي! خلاص هظْبُط الأجازة بُكْره و أشوف الحُجوزات.

A: I'm so fed up. I wish we could go away for a couple of days.
B: I'm all in! Just make the plans and tell me.
A: Okay, let's take Thursday off and go away Wednesday evening.
B: Perfect! All right. I'll arrange the time off tomorrow and see to the reservations.

لِمّ إيدك و لُسانك

Hey, watch it!

لِمّ إيدك و لُسانك [**lit.** restrain your hand and your tongue] is a warning to someone who is becoming abusive, swearing and hitting things. But if the person is only verbally (and not physically) aggressive, you would just say لِمّ لسانك.

أ: الله يْخَرِب بيْتك! إنْتَ عارِف المِرايَة اللي كسرْتهالي دي تمنْها كام؟
ب: لِمّ إيدك و لُسانك و اتْكلِّم بِأدب أحْسنْلك!
أ: ده أنا هوَدّيك في داهْيَة!
ب: شوف تمنها كام و أدْفعْهالك لكِن تِطوَّل لِسانك و تمِدّ إيدك يِبْقى نِطْلع عَ القِسْم و أنا اللي هوَدّيك في داهْيَة!

A: God damn you! Do you know how much that mirror you just broke cost?
B: You'd better restrain your hand and tongue and talk politely!

A: I'm going to give you hell!
B: Check how much it is, and I'll pay for it, but if you extend your tongue or hand, then we'll go to the police station, and I'll give YOU hell.

اللّه يْخرِّب بيْتك [lit. May God destroy your house]

وَدّى في داهْيَة [lit. to take to hell] to make pay, make trouble for

إيدي و رِجْلي

essential

إيدي و رِجْلي [lit. my hands and feet] represent something (or even someone) that is very important to you and you cannot do without.

أ: ما تْبيع يابْني العربية اللي مْغلِّباك دي.
ب: ما إنْتَ عارِف إنّها إيدي و رِجْلي، بَتْنقِّل بيها في شُغْلي و بَوَصَّل بيها المدام والولاد كلّ يوْم.

A: Why don't you sell this car that's causing you so much trouble, man?
B: You know it's my hand and foot. I use it to get around for my work and drive my wife and kids in it.

أ: مُمْكِن آخُد مِنَّك اللابْتوب بُكْره؟ بِتاعي في الصِّيانة و عنْدي بْرزنْتيْشن بُكْره؟
ب: للأسف أنا عنْدي تسْليمات كِتير كلّ يوْم. أنا مُصمِّم جْرافيك يابْني. اللابْتوب ده إيدي و رِجْلي.

A: Can I borrow your laptop tomorrow? Mine's in the shop, and I have a presentation.

B: Sorry, but I have a lot of work to deliver every day. I'm a graphic designer, dude. My laptop is my bread and butter.

أ: ما تْقولي لِأمّ مْحمّد تِبطّل تيجي السِّتّ كِبرِت في السِّنّ خالِص.

ب: حرام عليْكي يا بِنْتي! دي هيَّ إيدي و رِجْلي و مِش بَعْرِف أنْجِز حاجة في شُغْل البيْت مِن غيرْها. لَوْ كِبرِت في السِّنّ نِسْتحْمِلْها لكِن منقْطعْش عيشْها أبداً.

A: Why don't you tell Umm Mohamed to stop coming over [to clean]. The woman has really gotten old.

B: Shame on you [for saying that], daughter! She's my hands and feet. I can't get any housework done without her help. We'll put up with her, even if she's gotten old, but we will never cut off her livelihood.

عيْشُه [lit. *one's bread*] *one's livelihood, way of earning a living*

إيد وَرا و إيد قُدَّام

to come back empty-handed

إيد وَرا و إيد قُدَّام [lit. one hand back and another forward] **gives us the image of someone going with an empty hand and returning with an empty hand. It means** to come back empty-handed.

أ: لقيْتوا شقّة ولّا لسّه بتْدوّروا؟
ب: والله آدينا بنْنِزل كلّ يوْم نِشوف شقق بسّ مفيش حاجة مُناسْبة، كلّ يوْم نِرْجع إيد وَرا و إيد قُدَّام.

A: Have you found an apartment, or are you still looking?
B: Really, we go out every day looking at apartments, but there isn't anything suitable, and we come back every day empty-handed.

أ: شايْفاك راجِع إيد وَرا و إيد قُدَّام يَعْني.
ب: خيرْ فيه أيْه؟ كُنْتي عايْزة حاجة مِنّي؟
أ: يابْني، أنا مِش كلّمْتك قُلْتلك تِجيبْلي خُضْرة ضروري لِلمحْشي و إنْتَ راجِع؟

ب: آخ! نِسيت معلِشّ. طيِّب ثَواني هنْزِل أجيبْلِك على طول.

A: I see you've come back empty-handed!
B: So? Why? Did you need something from me?
A: Didn't I call you, son, and tell you to bring me herbs needed for the mahshy on your way back?
B: Oops! Sorry, I forgot. Okay, hold on, and I'll go get you some right away.

هشِمّ على ضهْر إيدي

How was I supposed to know?

شمّ على ضهْر إيدُه [lit. to smell on the back of one's hand] means to foresee (know something without evidence) and is usually found in the future tense as a rhetorical question: How was I supposed to know?

أ: مكانْش يِصحّ تِكلِّمْهُم دِلْوَقْتي و هُمّا عنْدهُم ضُيوف.

ب: و أنا هشِمّ على ضهْر إيدي إنّ عنْدهُم ضُيوف! أهُه اللي حصل بقى. هبْقى أكلِّمْهُم تاني بُكْره ولّا حاجة.

A: It wasn't appropriate for you to call them now when they have guests over.
B: How was I supposed to know that they had guests? It's just what happened. Then I'll call them tomorrow or whatever.

أ: محبكْش يَعْني تِتْكلِّمي عن هِديةْ عيد الأُمّ قُدّام سلْوى!

ب: طب أنا كُنْت هعْرف مِنيْن إنّ مامِتْها مُتَوَفِّية! مِش هشِمّ على ضهْر إيدي أنا!

أ: أنا كُنْت فاكْراكي عارْفة.

ب: لا لا يا بِنْتي، معْرِفْش والله.

A: Well, that wasn't necessary to talk about a Mother's Day gift in front of Salwa.

B: How could I have known that her mom had passed away! I couldn't have seen that coming!

A: I thought you knew.

B: No, dear, I didn't at all.

وِقِف على إيدُه

to wait and watch

[lit. stay/stand on one's hand] means to wait (rather than come back later) or watch (to make sure it is done right) while someone does a job for you.

أ: لازِم أجيب صنايْعية يِدّوا وِشّ نضافة لِلشُّقّة. شكْلها مِتْبهْدِل خالِص.

ب: أهمّ حاجة تُقف على إيديْهُم عشان يِعْمِلوا الشُّغْل مظْبوط.

A: I have to get some workers to give the apartment a fresh coat of paint. It looks so run down.
B: Most importantly, you have to keep an eye on them so the job gets done right.

أ: أنا مِحْتاجة أكْوي الطّرْحة دي بسّ خايْفة أحْرقْها.
ب: خلاص أدّيهالي أنزّلْها لِلمكْوَجي اللي تحْت، هأقف على إيدُه و أجيبْهالك على طول.

A: I need to iron this scarf, but I'm afraid I'll burn it.
B: Then give it to me, and I'll take it down to the ironing shop downstairs and wait while he does it, then bring it back to you right away.

اللي إيدُه في المايّة مِش زيّ اللي إيدُه في النّار

You don't get it!

[lit. he whose hands are in the water is not like one whose hands are in the fire**] is a proverb that implies that one cannot understand or sympathize with another's situation.**

أ: أنا مِش فاهْمة أيه الصُّعوبة فيه إنّك تسيبيه. إنْتي عارْفة إنّك مِش بِتْحِبّيه و مِش عارْفين تِقرّبوا مِن بعْض يِبْقى سيبيه طالما مفيش تفاهُم.

ب: اللي إيدُه في المايّة مِش زيّ اللي إيدُه في النّار. أنا خايْفة يْكون قراري غلط و خايْفة على مشاعْرُه جدّاً. و بيْني و بيْنِك مِش عايْزاها تيجي مِنّي.

أ: مِش صحّ كِده. لازِم تِحْسِمي المَوْقِف عشان وَقْتُكُم إنْتو الاِتْنيْن.

A: I can't understand what's so hard for you to break up with him. You know you don't love him, and you're not managing to get closer to each other, so leave him since you there's no chemistry.

B: He whose hands are in the water is not like one whose hands are in the fire. I'm afraid my decision will be a mistake, and I'm afraid his feelings will be hurt. And between you and me, I don't want it to come from my end.

A: That's not right. You have to settle the matter for [so you don't waste] both of your time.

Notice that the second half of this well-known proverb can be omitted.

أ: أنا اتْخنقْت مِن الشُّغْلانة المُقْرِفة دي.
ب: خلاص ما تِسْتقيل و تْريّح دِماغك.
أ: ما اللي إيدهُ في المايّة! و لمّا أسْتقيل يا فالح، أدْفع بقيةْ الأقْساط اللي عليّا مْنيْن؟

A: I have had enough of this sickening job.
B: Why don't you just quit and save yourself the headache?
A: He whose hands are in the water! [that is, 'You just don't get it.'] When I quit, smarty, how I'm I going to make my payments?

الإيد البطّالة نِجْسة

Idle hands are the devil's tool.

[lit. an idle hand is impure] is a proverb that expresses the value of working hard and not being lazy.

It can be used to encourage or criticize others.

أ: يابْني ما تْشوفْلك حاجة مُفيدة تعْمِلْها في الأجازة بدل ما إنْتَ قاعِد كده. ده حتّى الحركة بركة.
ب: أعْمِل أيْه يَعْني؟ ما هِيَّ أجازة!
أ: الإيد البطّالة نِجْسة يا حبيبي. يَلّا قوم شوف لَوْ فيه طلبات أمّك عايْزاها ولّا حاجة عايْزة تِتْصلّح.

A: Why don't you find yourself something useful to do during vacation instead of just sitting around like that. There's a blessing in moving.
B: What shall I do? It's vacation!
A: Idle hands are the devil's tool, honey. Come on, get up and see if your mom needs anything from the grocery store or if there's something that needs to be fixed.

It can also express one's pleasure or willingness to be busy.

أ: معْقولة يا طنْط، بِتِغْسِلي المَواعين مَيْصحِّش والله.

ب: يا بِنْتي فيها أيْه؟ ما أنا كِده كِده واقْفة في المطْبخ ده حتّى. الإيد البطّالة نِجْسة.

أ: لا يا طنْط مَينْفعْش والله روحي حضْرِتِك اِسْتِريّحي و أنا هغْسِلْهُم.

A: Come on, auntie! You're doing the dishes? That's totally unacceptable.

B: What of it, honey? I'm already standing in the kitchen, and idle hands are the devil's tool.

A: No way, auntie. This cannot happen. Just go relax, and I'll wash them myself.

lingualism

Visit our website for information on current and upcoming titles and free language learning resources.

www.lingualism.com